To the loveliest IT girl in the universe. So many thanks.

A Plain Man's Guide to The Asylum

Michael Gilderdale

Grosvenor House
Publishing Limited

This book is published by
Grosvenor House Publishing Ltd
28-30 High Street, Guildford, Surrey, GU1 3HY.
www.grosvenorhousepublishing.co.uk

A CIP record for this book
is available from the British Library

ISBN 978-1-906645-64-9

Acknowledgements

Thank you Faber & Faber Ltd., publisher of T. S. Eliot's poems, for permission to include lines from The Dry Salvages (Four Quartets) first published in 1944.

Thank you Routledge & Keegan Paul Ltd for quotations from Experiment in Depth, by P. W. Martin, first published in 1955

Also, a passing nod to friends various, those good companions who may find they appear in these marginal notes of social history.

Introduction

After toiling with words for former employers I have now found the time to put words on paper for myself in the form of this Journal. As mortals we are mostly made of water and words. It is unlikely that my words can do much harm. As for the water, I can only hope it will turn into wine.

Perhaps I should blame James Boswell. After reading his London Diary I was encouraged to write another of my own. James had a lively young mind as well as accepting an ambition to prove himself a success on the London scene in the mid 18th century. Well-born in Scotland, he hoped to do well among the titled and literate denizens of England's bursting capital with its great houses, its taverns and whorehouses. I am the reverse of James. He left Scotland for London, while I left London for Scotland. I should not compare myself to him, although we have something in common. He did not triumph in London, nor did I in Edinburgh, and we both had ill luck. He not infrequently suffered when catching the pox as a result of his amorous adventures, while I caught the disdain from others simply because I was an Englishman. The auld adversarial attitudes surfaced even though I kept a low profile and it would be no exaggeration to say that I was daily persecuted by a mad managing director who had engaged me to work in his company. Even the MD's own son was so similarly ill treated he sought sanctuary on the West coast of America and, as far as I know, never returned to his native Scotland.

There is of course one vast difference between Boswell's year in the London of his day, and my days north of The Border. He 'sauntered' about the streets and called upon fellow Scots, ate hearty meals and drank tea in favourite taverns where he sought discussion on the latest play or published tract. Thus his window on the world was confined to London where he dearly longed to join a regiment of Guards, but never managed to do so.

My window on the world is, inevitably, very different. I open it here on the last days of 2007.

Monday ◈ DECEMBER 24

Christmas Eve. I am filled with tenderness and compassion for our dogs. They are beautiful and have no knowledge of death, as far as I know. They show us astonishing affection. As well as half destroying the house.

Today, millions of people will be travelling to family or lovers. Just imagine, She tried phoning from Charles de Gaulle. "Darling where ARE you? I have waited all morning…an early flight you said. The boards simply repeat Delayed. Delayed. And now I have terrible fear, yes, I know it's irrational but in my heart I am not sure. Peut-etre you changed your mind? I cannot believe it. We will miss the last connection to Nice and you know we cannot stay in Rue Marveilleux. Vachement ! HE is still there, refusing to move and I am sure he suspects something. Darling, please, please hurry or I will die."

Desolate? Of course she is. No love. No Christmas stroll along the Rue des Anglais. No anything. Such disappointments are repeated by families, by illicit lovers, by cheats and criminals, by Nuns and Saints at airports, hotels and homes in Italy, in Spain and Portugal, even Sweden and Norway too. Why? Because the fog is down.

Planes grounded. It is reported. It is the reality. Thousands sleep beneath British Airways blankets at Gatwick, Heathrow, Manchester. Very few planes arrive or depart. A chill beginning to Christmas.

There is even less comfort and joy in North America's mid-West. From Texas to Minnesota the blizzard has brought a vast snowfall. Many thousands of homes without electricity. Road conditions unthinkable, as people die in accidents. Fifty lorries in TEXAS, domino fashion. Ah well, its just the usual festive season. Pain and rejoicing.

Here, we are lucky. Jenny has dashed off in the car with the dogs to buy bananas and collect smoked salmon as a present for her hairdresser. Perhaps when she returns we can have a quiet time until, I suspect, the carols at three p.m. I'm going to make soup. Vichyssoise. Then I'll watch rugby on TV. Leicester versus Sale Sharks. At 6.00p.m. we will visit H-W. He is being 65. Then supper, and at 10.30 p.m. we will go to the watch night service in Kilconquhar parish church before mulled wine and bed.

Tuesday ◆ DECEMBER 25

We may not do Christmas, and yet, and yet, we do 'tradition.' Last night, from 11.00 p.m. to midnight we sang our hearts out in the church. A full house. Ivy. Lanterns. The big illuminated stained glass window above the altar. It reminded me of John Betjeman. Minister Brian did the prayers.

This Christmas Day morning it was non-stop. Jenny chased off to Elie Kirk where she was doing the welcome. "Merry Christmas!" as she handed out carol sheets. I followed her into the church, which was packed out. More singing. Then the Minister engaged in conversation with the very young children who brought their presents to show him. And he showed them his presents. Amid gusts of laughter the familiar ritual continued. I found myself becoming stony-faced, although I confess Minister Brian did his part with warmth and kindness and truly Irish charm. Then, back to the cottage, a quick change of clothes and off helter-skelter to Jenny's nephew Peter for Bucks-Fizz and exchange of presents. THEN a breathless dash up the brae to Cadgers' Way, home of Mike and Dorothy Dickson, for Christmas lunch. Champagne, melon, turkey and ham a snowfield of boozy trifle and an excellent slice of hot pud.

Beneath the 12ft. tree lay a mass of presents all colourfully wrapped. Everyone gave and received. The family in full flood. Dorothy, Mike, Niall and Libby, Cally with her lover Colin (Irish Bank), Jennie (becoming a Lawyer), Julia known as 'Jools' very beautiful and unusually quiet, (second year Durham University), Bobby the Sheriff and son Graeme (a Lawyer), Andrew (Niall's son, becoming a criminal Lawyer). I had a great conversation with him and also with his Mother Libby who is a schools inspector. Husband Niall (formally BBC) is chief exec. of The King's Fund. Andrew is a star. He has worked among homeless children in the Far East and between his studies he does similar work in London.

We were back home by 4.30 p.m., then returned at 8.00p.m.

for turkey sandwiches and Christmas cake. So much food! Other visitors included Alastair Dickson and his wife Belinda the cashmere queen.

Wednesday ◈ DECEMBER 26

Boxing Day. The world and his wife are raiding the big stores for the bargains in the Sales. It is all part of the Winter Festival. And it is one reason why I feel unhappy at Christmas time. I wish we could separate the Christian celebration of Bethlehem from high street profit and human greed. Nae chance, laddie. I am obsessed by the thought that human life on this planet could so easily end tomorrow. Nuclear stockpiling. And it is not new. In 1962 I flew in a BOAC Comet over Cuba, and I took pictures of the Soviet Union's nuclear armaments below. A chance snapshot of the moment that the western world wobbled on the very edge of the abyss. A narrow escape from a nuclear holocaust. The Earth a burnt offering, by kind permission of Mankind.

Thursday ◈ DECEMBER 27

This evening with Jenny I will repair to the Golf House Club for her nephew Peter's 50th birthday party and sup and dance with about 80 other guests. That, apart from the forthcoming Hogmanay knees-up, will bring an end to all the feasting and drinking.

I should not grumble. Consider the millions on this benighted planet who have little or nothing to eat, not simply at Christmas time, but throughout the year. In Chad there are several million children dangerously deprived with many of them bought or sold for prostitution and abuse. And how many millions more in Africa will presently die of Aids, other diseases and tribal conflict.

Hardly had I completed this note than I learned that Benazir Bhutto had been shot and killed in Pakistan. The outcome is difficult to predict. More killings are likely. Pakistan is unstable at the best of times. America's Eastern ally is being attacked. Pakistan has a nuclear capability and is not surrounded by friends.

Statesmen around the world will make sympathetic noises. I have not felt comfortable through this Christmas.

Sunday ◆ DECEMBER 30

Morning Service and a baptism. Hymns that most of the congregation did not know and could not sing. That included me. I felt uneasy. Earlier, I should have been at the quiet Meeting for Worship in St. Andrews. Instead, I listened to a Service on Radio Four which came from a college at Durham University. The singing consisted of the earliest known carols, starting with The Boar's Head. It was explained that all carols were made to be sung AFTER Christmas rather than beginning at the end of November in supermarkets. The singing from Durham was terrific. Full-blooded. Here in the village, after the service church goers stepped across the road to the newsagent to get their papers. A pause from prayers to penny dreadfuls.

Monday ◆ DECEMBER 31

Que sera, sera. So, on New Year's Eve, concentrate on the Present. Optimism? Difficult. Looking Abroad – as we do – too many countries are bubbling with discontent and violence. Iraq. Afghanistan. The Middle East. Zimbabwe. Chad and the Sudan. The madness in Pakistan. And now, even Kenya. Riots and alleged vote rigging. Politics here at home? Rather a sorry mess. Never mind. A New Year is about to happen. Given the usual chicken, cheer, and kisses, things might improve. So – welcome 2008.

Tonight there will be the usual supper dance at the Club. Tables of 10 and perhaps a full house of 100.

A little sad humour might help. We have received a communication from Eric, a gnome of a millionaire who lives in Singapore and visits here once a year to see friends. He trawls the world and between June and October, 2008, will be giving birthday parties in Rome, London, Edinburgh, Amsterdam, Denver Colorado and Singapore. We feel we should go to the Edinburgh party. He gave one there five years ago, in Edinburgh Academy, his old school. This year his Christmas Card included ten jokes. I had better just try to start laughing.

And now I had better get ready. A walk with Jenny and the dogs across the links. Then a bath. Then a rest. Then black tie. Then to Alan and Sue. Then to Keith and Carolyn. Then to the Club. Food. Drink. Dance. Then the Bells. Then hugs and Kisses and the year's end. Goodbye 2007.

Seated at Table 7 with Jenny and I were Alan and Jen Corbett, Carolyn and Keith, Robert and Eileen Burns and Marcia and Ian Ritchie. We consumed rather too many bottles of red and white wine to accompany the Woodwards buffet that stretched the length of the main club corridor. Elrick's Band played. The decibels rose and most of the company present did too as they slid, shuffled and leapt around the dance floor until midnight. It was a modest celebration compared to the streets of London which, it was reported, were thronged by hundreds of thousands of citizens beneath cascades of fireworks. Ambulances were dealing with 500 casualties per hour, while 3,600 police officers patrolled the streets.

Hogmanay and New Year's Day were rather different in 1763 according to James Boswell in London. On Friday December 31st he wrote "I waited on Louisa. The conversation turned upon love, whether we would or not." On January 1st the affair grew warmer. "Nay Sir, you are an encroaching creature!" (Upon this I advanced to the greatest freedom by a sweet elevation of the charming petticoat).

'Good Heaven, Sir!' "Madam I cannot help it. I adore you. Do you like me?" (She answered me with a warm kiss, and pressing me to her bosom, sighed, 'O Mr Boswell!') "But my dear Madam ! Permit me, I beseech you." 'Lord, Sir. The people may come in.' "How then can I be happy? What time? Do tell me." 'Why, Sir, on Sunday afternoon my landlady of whom I am most afraid, goes to church, so you may come here a little after three.'

So, three it was! Mission no doubt accomplished!

Tuesday ◆ JANUARY 1, 2008

AN EXTREME PILGRIM

We were a-bed by 1.30 this morning and woke early to the barking of Millie and Gemma. By 11.30 we were watching, on TV, the annual concert from Vienna, the Philharmonic being conducted for the first time by a Frenchman, Georges Pretre. And we were enchanted, as were one billion other people around the world by the avalanche of Strauss family waltzes and polkas, and the brilliant ballet, including the disciplined dancing of the snowy Lipizzaner horses. At 7.30 p.m. We go to The Kineuchar Inn for supper with the golden oldies.

Wednesday ◆ JANUARY 2

Jenny presented me with a sleeveless jerkin. A New Year present. According to the label it was made from 7 recycled plastic bottles. (quote): "The process means crushing and heating the bottles to a high temperature to produce fibres, which make yarn. Good for you. Good for the environment. "

Last evening I was NOT bottled (in the alcoholic sense) and there were only about 30 oldies for supper. As ever, the event was organised in the Pub by Harry and Mae Noble. Big Harry is as tall as the beams overhead. Mae still has an arm in a sling. They both slipped and fell in the driveway of their house and would still be lying there had not someone spotted them. She was injured and, in any case could not have lifted Harry because he is a giant. If it happened again I fear the Council would have to get a crane to the rescue.

Now, it is time for mulled wine, and letters to write. Out on the windy links, under an overcast sky, men are playing the traditional shotgun competition called The Hangover Cup. (I won it one year because I was partnered by Jimmie McQuarry who was strong, long and patient).

Thursday ◆ JANUARY 3

Part the curtains and the windows are lighter. Crescent moon and morning star shine brightly as a weary world drags itself back to work, with snow forecast for Scotland. But as the wind whines and rises to punish bushes and creep under doors we strive to keep hope alive, despite gloomy and rather odd news. It seems this is The Year of The Frog. Around the world the many species of frog are dying as a result of a fungal condition which blocks their skin (through which frogs breathe). So, they suffocate. This is worrying because, if frogs disappear the mosquitoes on which they live will thrive and spread malaria.

More immediately, in America the Iowa caucasus happens today with only about 15 per cent. of voters likely to be active, so who can tell which of the Democratic and Republican contenders will win through? Add to that the fact that the tribal war in Kenya is worsening and you have good grounds for becoming a Class One pessimist.

I rang Owen (brother) in York on Boxing Day. His speech was halting and blurred. This morning Alan (brother in New Zealand) rang me to say he had heard Owen was in hospital. I have just called York. He is still in hospital and very unwell with Parkinson's.

Friday ◈ JANUARY 4

Holy Moses! Now, Jenny's sister is ill 'in bed with the doctor.' And the dogs cannot get their morning walk yet because it is raining stair-rods. I turn on the radio and find that the BBC is clearly going down the tubes. Even when interviewers and interviewees get to the mike they speak so badly that the word gobbledegook comes to mind. Thankfully, James Naughty and John Humphries are audible and highly professional. Naughtie gave the caucus news today. For the Republicans the Godly Mike Huckabee and warrior McCain should come through, and for the Democrats Barack Obama and Hilary Clinton will make it to New Hampshire.

Saturday ◈ JANUARY 5

Constance, who edits the Tayside Quaker, has asked me to write a short comment on Last night's TV documentary called 'Extreme Pilgrim.' So this morning I have mailed the following to her:- 'In the first of three TV programmes Peter Owen-Jones, a C of E Vicar, demonstrates how to "shed the load of modern life." In his journey to the Buddhist Monks of central China he experiences the extreme pain of martial arts and attempts the "non attachment" of Zen in monasteries amidst the ravishing beauty of the mountains. He learns that true peace is gained through extreme physical pain and rhythmical, flowing movements. Release yourself from Life's problems, he is told. Become one with nature, witness the way the wind caresses a bush and note how the birds circle and lean on the wind. Make peace with yourself, renounce the earthly world. Integrate breathing, movement and silence. Christians are too deeply attached to "everything, including family and children."

In attempting the Monks' severe disciplines Peter found he was" not missing alcohol, meat and Pepsi." Equally, he confessed "I am gaining no spiritual insights here, I am in a goldfish bowl." However, the young students he was with will return to the world of telegrams and anger very fit in body and mind and thus acquire spiritual health.

The programme was compelling. Peter Owen-Jones was an advertising exec. before becoming a Vicar with three parishes in the Sussex Downs, and currently he still does alcohol and nicotine. As an 'Extreme Pilgrim' he comes face to face with 1,500 years of tradition. There are 30,000 martial arts students in China. Peter learns that martial arts is a release of energy but in it "there is stillness." He found the practice a total agony. He became sick and reached a point where he could take no more. Encouraged to meditate he found that he kept thinking of his cat and his children on playground slides. But, at least he opened himself to spiritual experiment. It involved making an eight-hour journey from Beijing to beautiful but dizzying mountains 5,500 ft high and a complete community of smiling, affectionate but non homosexual Monks. It was all "totally alien from anything we in the West have and do." In the course of his initiation a friendly Monk diagnosed that Peter was suffering from a variety of infections and illnesses.

Sunday ◆ JANUARY 6

Me too! I appear to have collected one of the popular bugs currently infecting the good people of this place. After monumental sneezing I have had to spend the morning in bed with no voice, streaming nose and eyes and a cough louder than both dogs barking. Jenny is still standing, but she had her bout of the bug a few weeks ago. And, it was ironic. She had given up her church duties today to drive me to Meeting in St. Andrews, and now I can't go. Through the windows the sun in a blue sky is blinding and as bright as a June day. Someone called this phenomenon 'A January smile.' Grounded, I listened to a radio programme featuring the son of R.D. Laing, the famous and infamous psychologist/psychiatrist, adulterer and alcoholic. Did he really contribute to the happiness of the human condition?

John Humphries, on Desert Island Discs, said that when doing interviews he had been frightened of only two women – Margaret Thatcher and the great Ella Fitzgerald. Well, I also interviewed Ella (in The Savoy Hotel, London), and she was lovely. We drank orange juice, but when I had the cheek to ask if she would care to sing one of her timeless songs (why not ' Stompin at The Savoy', or better still Cole Porter's 'Everytime we Say Goodbye') she declined. One of her minders explained that she only sang when giving a concert in public.

This afternoon Jean Glen rang to ask if we would return the dog cage she lent us, as her son David, on the farm up at Errol, had three parrots who had grown too large for their current abode!

Monday ◈ JANUARY 7

I am ill. But the misery has not prevented my dreams. Last night I lay with Jenny on a bed that was outside a house. I gazed into her eyes and asked ' Do you still want to wear your engagement ring?' She smiled up at me and answered yes. 'And do you still want to wear your wedding ring?' Answer: 'Yes, of course I do.'

When I awoke I felt I was the happiest man alive. On reflection, however, I fear my questions suggest shocking insecurity.

Tuesday ◈ JANUARY 8

Heavy rain and a Force 10 forecast kept me grounded until 2.30 p.m. today. Jenny served up a magnificent broth composed of all the left-over veg she could find, and some energy returned. The bedside radio gave me the story of a favourite song – 'New York, New York.' A famous Welsh male voice choir was booked to give a concert in New York when disaster struck. Nine Eleven. The twin towers. The choir debated whether to travel to the US. Danger or not they voted unanimously to go. They were booked into Carnegie Hall but, checking on the spot discovered that only the first two rows in the auditorium would be filled. On advice the choir leader chose TV to tell New York that the choir had come over specially to show sympathy with the city. By the time the choir performance opened the great Carnegie Hall was booked out. Capacity. When the choir ended its performance with New York, New York, the clapping began, the stamping, the singing, the dancing is the aisles. Tears as well as cheers.

Today it's the New Hampshire Primary. Maybe there will be more dancing in the aisles when the result comes through. Obama or Hillary?

Wednesday ◆ **JANUARY 9**

Last night gales of 80 and 90 mph plagued Scotland. Some roads and bridges have been closed. Lorries overturned. Trees and power lines down. Flooding, and many homes without electricity. Here, on our exposed hillside we took a battering. Such was the noise that we could not sleep. Gemma barked. Millie leapt on and off our bed, completely spooked, while I choked, coughed and sweated. At 2.00 a.m. Jenny, bless her cotton socks, made a cup of tea.

So, how about New Hampshire. Surprise, surprise. All the polls (and me) got it wrong. Hillary Clinton narrowly defeated Obama. She told her supporters – mainly women –"I listened to you, and I found my voice." And the Republicans ? McCain. Also narrowly. On the long road to The White House no doubt more surprises lie in wait. Thank goodness for books to read. I have just encountered Boswell listening to the "stupendous" Johnson. (Quote):

"Political institutions are formed upon the consideration
of what will most frequently tend to the good of the

whole, although now and then exceptions may occur. It is better in general that a nation should have a supreme legislative power, although it may at times be abused. But, then, there is this consideration: that if the abuse be enormous, Nature will rise up, and claiming her original rights, overthrow a corrupted political system."

I wonder what Dr. Johnson would have made of some political systems today. Zimbabwe. Pakistan. Afghanistan, Iraq. Burma. Nairobi. The Sedan.

Thursday ◆ JANUARY 10

At 7.30 a.m. Jenny went out (with the dogs) and so did the lights. Power cut. I found six candles.

After eight days of miserable health I gave in today and went to the Surgery. The lady doctor Wilson is young and lively with smiles that are not simply a professional façade. So – antibiotics.

I accompanied Jenny to Paw Prints, a kennels in the midst of nowhere. They are large and new and will be a great help to our dogs when we have to leave home for a night or a fortnight. Before supper Judy Mason called in with a note from David, and two gifts. A charming dish named Garlic Bread, and a bottle of 'Reading Room Claret', a Faculty of Advocates tipple. A case of the Claret had been given to David by his son Andrew who is becoming a criminal lawyer. David's note included two quotes I relish. One from H.L. Menken said: "The urge to save humanity is almost always a false front for the urge to rule." The second quote is his own. "Remember," he says, "A pessimist is an optimist who has all the facts."

Friday ◆ January 11

Ed Hilary has died in Auckland NZ. His Everest triumph with sherpa Tensing was announced the day the Queen was crowned, and my task as a young journalist was to write and report on the Royal processions for my newspaper. I was stationed on a roof in The Mall and instructed to phone my copy from a telephone exchange in Green Park. At the end of a long day I found the exchange, but no one had shown me how to work the manual switchboard. I had a limited 'window' in which get my copy through in time to make the first edition. In the end I managed to get the correct plug in the right hole - a close call. I also had to attend the Garden Party at Buckingham Palace where Tensing and Hilary would be guests of honour. There was no chance of a proper interview. It rained cats and dogs so my 'story' had to be how the two heroes had brought a torrential monsoon from Nepal to SW1.

Today I am preparing for tomorrow's Monks' Festival in Edinburgh's Royal College of Surgeons. I am expected to have a 'contribution' (ie - verses) and will do a short nonsense called 'Time for Tea' with a chorus which I trust all present will join in. (quote) Hoolungooree, that's for me ! Exceptionally rare Assam tea !

Saturday ◆ JANUARY 12

TV's Extreme Pilgrim, Peter Owen-Jones, made a second journey "to find one-ness with God." It takes him to the great Hindu festival beside the waters of the River Ganges attended by a mind-boggling seven million worshipers. Here, he seeks to explore the minds of those who have renounced the material world, and says "it will help my understanding of God."

In the vast, tented city beside the waters he finds 13 different orders of Holy men and their followers and seeks to don the role of a Saddhu (Holy man) himself. He finds it an alien, intimidating world, but he is genuinely welcomed. He dons the colourful robes and beads, and sits with the Holy leaders as they smile, chant and sing, smoke their hash and accept gifts of money which they then give away. He confesses "I do not know where I am!"

The great, wide Ganges is the meeting point between Heaven and Earth. The vast throngs run as if crazed to the waters edge. Many are stripped naked and covered in ash. Into the water they go, splashing, ducking and playing around like joyful children on a summer's outing.

Afterwards, Owen-Jones takes a second journey of two days to a Holy city and finds that "everywhere there is God." He also journeys to the high mountains to seek purity and learning, and experiences a letting go of desire and self and fear. His final step is a 12-hour bus ride to the foothills of the Himalayas. Here above a village he finds a Holy man's cave, cleans it out and remains there for a week. The villagers bring him all he needs to sustain life. Treating him as a Saddhu they ask him to bring them much-needed rain. They also ask him to bless a man's daughter. And then alas his physical journey comes to an abrupt end. He contracts dysentery, is very ill and confesses "I can go no further." The fact is he has gone a long way, the hard way to find a oneness with God. Truly he has been at one with all those he meets in a journey of Faith, open-ness, pain and courage that few from an indulgent Western world would ever contemplate.

Today its the annual Monks Festival in the Surgeons' Hall. But first we had to take Millie and Gemma to kennels for 24 hours. We then drove to Edinburgh to collect my Monks gown from the Chapter House and then proceed to 11 A Hope Terrace where we will stay for the night when the Festival ends at around 11 p.m. This is the home of Gavin and Margot Anderson. It is a beautiful house, listed, and excellently re-modelled by Margot and Gavin (with a little professional help).

Gavin returned from shooting pheasant in Perthshire. We drank a glass of wine, then changed into our DJ's and gowns and drove over to the Surgeon's Hall. Sherry was served in the ante-room to the Library where the tables had been set with 44 place settings. Some of The Second Fifteen Monks had invited guests who might have a verse or two to read to us from the lectern. I was seated near the end of Gavin's table – he being The Fiscal and responsible for fining Fathers who had misbehaved. The old Prior, young Papageno, was, as custom decreed, replaced by Father Botulus. Later I was called to do my verse, and I was aided by two Varlets who held a scroll of paper above my head inscribed with the words of my chorus for all to see and to join me in shouting. There were some good verses from both guests and Fathers, but on the whole I found it quieter and less joyful than previous Festivals. However, I had the comfort of Father Akros on my left, Father Seneca on my right and Hannibal opposite. At 11.15 Jenny called and drove Gavin and I back to 11A for a taste of Armagnac and bed.

Sunday ◈ JANUARY 13

We collected Millie and Gemma from the kennels. Mrs Peebles, the kennel mistress, was in her house with babe in arms. Our two very wet and muddy dogs were produced (they had been on a walk over the fields) and we returned home. We cleaned them and all was quiet. The dogs were tired, and so were we. However, Jenny insisted on watching, on TV, the first episode of Lark Rise to Candleford, and the last episode of Jane Austen's Sense and Sensibility. Close-ups of lovely faces under silly bonnets, floods of emotion, anger, disappointment, whispered intimacies, kisses and embracing AND of course, carriages, cottages, country mansions and cobbles, plus – inevitably – elegant Balls and bastards. I find myself admiring the casting, some of the performances and, above all, the research, AND the property department which ensures authenticity of every object from a penned letter to a plate on table or dresser.

Monday ◈ JANUARY 14

An early start, to take Gemma to the vets. She has to be 'spayed' as we alas do not want more pups. We then drove over to St. Andrews. There, the traffic problem gets steadily worse and the pavements are thronged. The University is back I think. Cheerful First Year girls stride out, many of them wearing identical light blue bottom-shaping jeans with knee-length boots. Plain Jane's and pretty Lucindas, heads full of hope and wickedness, chatter along, condoms safely in back pockets. After all, Uni is not just medicine and mathematics. It is an early stage of the mating game. This afternoon Jenny has gone to her Monday Bridge. At 4.00 p.m. I will ring the vet for news of Gemma. Meantime, Millie, who has been watching me through the open study door, has just been sick on the hall carpet. She was sick again. And then a third time. When Jenny returned from her bridge we went to the vet to bring Gemma home. Poor lamb, she could hardly walk and was still half asleep. Jenny tucked her into her cage and we hope she will sleep all night. Meantime it became clear that Millie really is unwell.

Tuesday ◈ JANUARY 15

We were lucky to get any sleep last night. Gemma cried a lot and banged about, her 'lampshade' clattering against the wire walls of her cage. Millie lay most of the night in the hall, not on her bed. After breakfast we rang the Vet. The surgery was very busy and could not see Millie until 3.00 p.m. I said that was too late, so finally the nurse said "Well bring her in at 10 a.m. but we can't look at her until mid afternoon at the earliest."

We then had, to visit H. Samuels at The Kingdom Centre in Glenrothes to check a signet ring to replace the one I lost in Yorkshire. We found nothing suitable, so we hurried back home to a distressed Gemma. In our absence the Vet had rung to say he would ring again later to report on Millie. This he did, but it was not good news. She is in a similar state to the time several months ago when she had to have her tummy opened and cleared of some substance or object she had eaten. If this turns out to be the case again she will have to suffer a second operation, then come home and the two of them will each have a lampshade. That spells chaos. However, with luck she might recover overnight.

Wednesday ◈ JANUARY 16

We anxiously await news from the Vet. I fear Millie may have to be opened up again. We will have a problem. Gemma is currently going mad with the irritation of her wound one minute and passing out the next. Under the Vet's advice we are having to dope her down every 24 hours.

I am still reeling from our visit to The Kingdom in Glenrothes yesterday to inspect a signet ring. The shopping mall is actually Hell on Earth.

I have written to the Rev. Ian Paton to wish him well after his heart by-pass operation. Doing so reminds me again of The Church of Christ. I think it was a Bishop or Minister in London who said the Churches pews were filling with Christians from many lands overseas (ie: immigrants) rather than home-grown Christians. He commented on this as a good thing. But has he paused to consider what the flood of immigrants is doing to the country? The Church, of course, has to welcome all comers, saints and sinners alike. But at what price? Urban areas are over-populated and there is an urgent need for more houses to be built. Even in non-urban areas the roads are over-crowded with too many vehicles and the jams and tail-backs will increase.

The Vet phoned to say they are keeping Millie for the day, but hoping not to have to operate. It all depends on whether she will eat. They have done a blood test which shows a normal result. We are to ring the Vet at 5.00p.m. for further news. So we rang. The Vet is keeping Millie until she takes food and water.

Thursday ◆ JANUARY 17

The abominable weather keeps us indoors with lights on even at 10.30.a.m. Jenny is doing a wonderful job nursing Gemma who alternates between crying and crashing from room to room in an agony of pain and or irritation from her wound.

Yesterday, being housebound I read a little from a book titled 'Spilling the Beans.' It is the autobiography of Clarissa Dickson Wright of TV's 'Two Fat Ladies' fame. After becoming what Lord Denning termed a very promising young Lawyer, Clarissa became an heroic alcoholic after the death of her mother. After inheriting about £2 million she blew the lot, became homeless, finally gave up alcohol and became a Celeb and of course a remarkable cook.

Jenny worked for her father Dickson Wright at his clinic in Lister House, Wimpole Street, London and was there about the time I first met her. DW was a noted cancer surgeon. He spent much of his time raising money for what was then called The Imperial Cancer Research Fund. He careered around town crash-ing his Jaguar as he visited pubs to pick up collecting boxes. Jenny and nurses from St. Mary's Hospital were also fund-raisers and shook tins at First Nights in the West End Theatres. Her father was a friend of 'Dickie' DW and a patron of the Fund. In the library of the Royal College of Surgeons (London) there is plaque which reads "This room is named in recognition of the special services of W. Arnold Innes."

'Dickie' did not like me because he realised when I married

Jenny she would no longer be his aid. Who would then collect his crashed cars around London? As for Clarissa, I remember her here in Scotland as a cook for charity Balls when our Band played for the dancing.

At 5.00p.m. we rang the Vet and had encouraging news. Millie is doing well, eating a little and looking better. With any luck we might get her home tomorrow.

Friday ◆ JANUARY 18

This morning we collected a very quiet Millie. She is still eating very little chicken and rice and must be fed three or four times a day. Gemma, still wearing her lampshade, is in her cage for a while.

Saturday ◆ JANUARY 19

Extreme Pilgrim Peter Owen-Jones, on TV last night, set out in Egypt with the aim of re-living the experience of the early Christian hermits. His starting point was Cairo, city of 1,000 mosques, but his interest was to get into the mind of St. Anthony who went into the desert 1,800 years ago. In AD 251 St. Anthony took a boat across the river to start his spiritual journey, so Peter, in AD 2008 did the same. His first stop was an underground shrine where St. Anthony had spent 20 years training for the journey to come. Peter remained underground briefly before setting out across the desert on a camel, guided by tent-dwelling Bedouin Arabs to distant mountains and the Monastery of St. Anthony. The Bedouins were delightfully conversational. "If God wishes we will have more camels," said one. Another said he would prefer a car. Another said "I ask only that God shelters me." He asked Peter to tell them which was the best day in his life so far. Peter replied "The day I was married." That is the best, the Arabs agreed. But Peter had to add that he is now separated from his wife and children, "and that hurts."

After arriving at the Monastery the Arabs left. Peter described the Monastery as the oldest in the world. "Christianity came here in the 1st century." At the foot of the mountains it was, surprisingly, a green place, with palm trees and a running stream. He found the Monastery "very beguiling, almost mystical." There were 100 Monks, and he saw them in prostration and prayer. (I found it remarkably modern with a metalled road and crosses on the top of two towers, brightly lit by neon tubes). Peter's next stop was to be a cave, high in the dusty, barren mountains. A solitary Monk, Fr. Lazarus, showed him the way. Lazarus looked like a bearded Old Testament prophet, but his hands were spotless and he spoke better English than most of Peter's Sussex parishioners.

Peter's cave was well equipped with food (I swear I saw a jar of Nescafe) and he remained there for three weeks with a camera and mike to record his thoughts. He prays. It is such a quiet place, he says, that "you could hear a lump of sugar dissolving in a cup of coffee." As he stalks about he sings "One Man went to mow", and "There were ten green bottles." He also says "I just want to go home. I see no purpose in a loving God. There is definitely a dark place, the eternal battle." In the end he said "I am beginning to come alive again, like being born." He was ready to face "another beautiful day".

It was all very odd, and I did not feel that his Egypt experience, or his visits to India and China earlier had really changed him. He realised his duty was to live among people and serve them. Surely that was what he had been doing, as a Vicar, before he set out on his extreme pilgrimage.

Back in China PM Gordon Brown is now in Shanghai looking for business deals for Britain and being closely shadowed by Sir Richard Branson hoping for a deal on Northern Rock. But there is more bad luck shadowing Brown. Back home, a laptop has been stolen from a car belonging to a Naval officer. It contains details of 600,000 Services recruits and potential recruits, many personal details including Bank accounts, passports etc. This about the fourth batch of sensitive material to go missing in the last month or two.

Sunday ❖ JANUARY 20

To Quaker Meeting in St. Andrews. A square, well-carpeted room with comfortable chairs set around a small round table on which there are several books, including 'Advices and Queries.' A tumble of ferns from a mantelshelf. About 30 Friends and visitors attending. Stillness. Silence for one hour as usual. Coffee in the library afterwards. After some absence I was greeted with hugs and kisses. Amazing. Jenny attended her Church of Scotland Service, this time in Kilconquhar Kirk, with the Moderator visiting. Returning home we invited David and Sheila to look in for pre-lunch drinks.

Monday ❖ JANUARY 21

Trivia today, and I keep thinking of William Wordsworth at Dove Cottage who complained, to Dorothy no doubt, about the mundane chores he had to face. He has my sympathy. We are all waiting for the daffodils. It is difficult to keep drab thoughts at bay, especially after reading the Sunday Times Magazine's feature on Trident Submarines. The courage of the crew is never in doubt. Imagine being submerged for three months at a time with nuclear warheads for company which, if used, have a range of 4,000 miles and, from mid-Atlantic, could devastate much of Eastern Europe and The Middle East. They can in fact wipe out entire countries. The Tridents have a limited life, but to replace the four that Britain possesses would cost between £15 billion to £20 billion. That's rather a lot of dosh which I personally believe could be better used. But, what's new? For 50 years a handful of countries have possessed the capability of destroying much of life on Earth. The text continues "Now a new, super-rich Russia is planning to re-equip its navy with nuclear subs, China is expanding its navy, and Iran is determined to get nuclear weapons."

This morning we took Gemma to the Vet for (hopefully) a final inspection of her wound/scar. All is well and she is now back to her determination to destroy not simply the odd table but the entire house!

Tuesday ❖ JANUARY 22

A busy day for Jenny. Off to the Club at 9.45 a.m. to play another Winter Foursomes Tie with Susie. There is snow on the Lammermuirs but the course is open and the air is still after a ribbed, blood-red curtain was drawn across the sky. Is it some kind of warning? No matter, the Ladies play golf in all weathers. Gnarled, tough as old boots, triple-baked and chattering. Jenny will return around 2.30 p.m. then exit again later to have supper in the Clubhouse and listen to Suzy Delaney explaining the benefits of Pilates. Jenny knows all about it, as she attends the Pilates class once a week. Busy. Busy. That is Jenny's preference. Golf. Ladies' Handicap Secretary. Regular Church with Elders' duties. massage AND Pilates. Dog walking. Shopping. The evening meal.

Wednesday ◆ JANUARY 23

Money markets in turmoil in Japan, London and especially New York, but things are said to be improving and Britain will be better placed than most to ride the storm. Even so, The Bank of England says a real recession here is a distinct possibility. The cost of houses here is still daft. A new build in South Street will probably cost half a million, but that is nothing compared with the cottage in Chapel Green which has been 'removed' to make room for a new house on the tiny site with a sea view. The old house and small site sold for about £1 1/4 million. Even the top flat at Earl-sneuk, near by, is priced at nearly £1 million.

Our financial transaction today is simple. Jenny is off to the village. I have given her £2.00 to purchase two kippers with their heads on. Now, I had better ring Angela at The Quinta do Lago Country Club (Algarve) to see if they have sold our remaining time-share week there. At £7,000 net (all taxes paid) it could buy quite a lot of kippers.

It is time to get angry with Sky TV. To report a plane crash, or the political scene, or global financial troubles is responsible and respects the viewers' understanding and intelligence. BUT to report (as Sky does) the crazy saga of the abducted Madeleine, of the long past death of Diana Princess of Wales, of a man who jumped from a balcony in Crete with his kids, and the unexpected death of a Hollywood star is a total BORE. Sky News is now filling the screen with stories that are years old.

Thursday ❖ JANUARY 24

Darkness covers the Earth. Lights on to defeat the gloom. Candles to light when there is a power cut. In darkness Faith seems to take a battering. Faith demands courage. Who likened the acceptance of Faith to walking a tightrope stretched across Niagara Falls. Dare you step onto that thin, swaying rope and set out for the far bank, and is there rescue if you fall?

The global warming debate will not leave us. Wiseacres are none too cheerful as we face a catch twenty two situation. The West has to cut back on economic growth to lessen the emission of those toxic carbons up to the ozone layer. Is there a Government that dare legislate for less rather than more economic development which adds to global warming.

I feel ' Black Dog,' as Winston Churchill would have said on a bad day. But—now, here is a better thought. Jane Carstairs (Grey Eyes) has just rung up to invite us to a Burns Supper with friends at her home in South Street. Tomorrow. Do a bit of tartan, she said. And what about a verse. Husband Jim will do the address to the Haggis.

Blimey, it IS a black day – at least for Peter Hain. With the Police and the Electorate Commission on his tail he had to resign for not declaring, at the time, some £103,000 of the £106,000 donated to his campaign to become Deputy Prime Minister of the Labour Party. His resignation from the Department of Work and Pensions, and as Secretary of State for Wales leaves a big Cabinet role to be filled and casts yet another shadow on Gordon Brown's ability to keep his Party in order.

Friday ❖ JANUARY 25

We are off to St Andrews for lunch, followed by a visit to the dentist, followed by a visit to the oculist to have my eyes checked, followed by shopping. Later to Grey Eyes' Burns Supper. I will take a couple of verses to read. For the Monks' monthly chapters over 21 years I have written some 201 verses. Add to that other songs and/or verses I have done. Well, it's an awfu' lot of nonsense.

It was a great party. I will write a thank you to Jim and Grey Eyes tomorrow, as we did not get to bed until after midnight.

Saturday ◆ JANUARY 26

"Dear Grey Eyes,

Come candlelight and show to me those friendly complexions again!

We were aye soncy last night to be 'blythe wi' comrades dear.' and hasten to say our thanks. We had the courtesy of your lovely home and of yourselves – and as for celebrating The Man, well, no one could do it better. Jim's conversation wi' the meat was spoken with a poetic lilt, such charm and style, even tenderness, and this was reflected in the wonderful refection. Small wonder we were loth to leave the table! Murray was quietly naughty amang the corn rigs. I fear I was a swasher with stuff that was terribly un-Scottish.

We enjoyed excellent company and meeting new people was part of the total refreshment. It was a memorable evening for us and, as we remarked as we tumbled into bed, we have never seen Grey Eyes and Jim in such sweet harmony. Truly you are in your prime.

Thank you!"

Having put the above in an envelope it was time to get on with the day. Leaving the dogs locked in the house we drove over to North Queensferry for lunch. Alan and Jen Corbett had recommended that we try The Wee Restaurant. We found it almost directly beneath the north bank arch of the railway bridge. A plain interior, small, with white washed walls and stout, serviceable tables and chairs. Jenny ordered a pate for starter while I had a great bowl of moules with pine nuts in a wonderful soup. When I had devoured the mussels the large linen napkin I had been given was whisked away and replaced with another. We then both had guinea fowl served with potatoes and pancetta. All washed down with a glass of South African blanc and some sparkling water. With service added the lunch cost £20 per head. We felt the wee place would do well for lunch on Friday when Jim and Barbara come up from Buckinghamshire for the Saturday international at Murrayfield.

I should have noted earlier that the verses I read for the Burns Supper were called 'Slainte' (in praise of whisky), and 'A vegetable Love.' The latter was one of several songs I wrote for Peter Gordon to set to music.

Sunday ◈ JANUARY 27

Today is Holocaust Day when the Jewish people ask us never to forget the millions of ordinary, innocent families who were slaughtered by the Nazis. I do not forget. I visited the Belsen Concentration Camp just after it was 'liberated' by the Allied Forces. Since that time many hundreds of millions have been slaughtered in many different countries around the world – much of it due to tribal warfare. Man's inhumanity to Man continues, and knows no end.

Jenny left for the church where she was to read one of the Lessons "I will lift up mine eyes to the hills whence cometh my help?"

I was not feeling up to lifting my eyes anywhere, but decided to drive over to Friends Meeting in St. Andrews. I was early. Ursula and Leslie were setting out cups and biscuits from the smart kitchen so that Friends and visitors could have coffee or tea after the Meeting which lasts one hour. After 40 minutes or so in silence one of the elders rose to her feet and spoke. A little later Barbara and Leslie 'Ministered.' I could not hear what any of them said, as they mumbled, or whispered. I do wish Friends would speak up. I am sure I am not the only person there who could not hear.

A very mixed bunch of people attend Quaker Meetings – just as church congregations also are like liquorice all-sorts. and over coffee and a biscuit I try to speak with people attending whom I do not know. Today I found myself in conversation with a tall girl. I asked what her trade was and she said she had been a nanny to a variety of families but was now a primary school teacher. I liked her. She was sunny.

Monday ◈ JANUARY 28

I feel guilty, having done little more than write letters and read a few more pages of 'Spilling the Beans,' the book by Clarissa Dickson-Wright that we were given for Christmas. I knew she was a reformed alcoholic but not that she and the other Fat Lady, Jennifer, were both Roman Catholics. It was however, pure chance that they met and could never have dreamed that their mad TV series would be translated into most of the world's languages, including the one that the Esquimos speak.

Tuesday ◈ JANUARY 29

Rain. Rain. Jenny and dogs drenched from their walk. Outlook dismal. I wrote a piece for Constance (Tayside Quaker) which was an edited extract from my brother Alan's essay on Quakers and The Arts. Brother Owen is still in hospital – he has had a brain scan so I will telephone later today to learn the result.

Mid way through the afternoon the door bell rang and there on the threshold was Brian McDowell, the Minister from the church in the village. He has been here in this living since last July. He is tall, very friendly with a Northern Irish brogue and was the former Chaplain at Fettes College in Edinburgh. Jenny offered him coffee and he sat with us for a while. He is wonderful company and we are most fortunate to have him. Before he left we had a wee prayer, and even the dogs, as well as ourselves, behaved respectfully. I like him. He is very fond of Jenny and wishes all his Elders were as good as 'wonderwoman.'

I rang for news of Owen. Tony said he has been very, very ill, but is coming through the worst of it. The results of the brain scan are not up yet.

Wednesday ◈ JANUARY 30

Jenny drove off to her Pilates class. Before leaving she gave me five leeks which meant only one thing – I was to make leek and potato soup. I used pheasant stock that she had kept in the fridge. Soup-making for Winter months should really be done in a vast pot on an old fashioned kitchen range and kept bubbling away day and night, and regularly refreshed with vegetables, left-over meat and the bones you didn't give to the dogs.

Tonight we are bidden for supper with Valerie Oliphant, an ancient friend of Jenny's family. There will be memories of London days. A book review in last Sunday's Culture magazine indicates that nowadays we do not know what we are eating, such are the extra items that are inserted into many foods. Examples are Battery chickens (such as those you might purchase at the supermarket). They contain three times more fat than they did 30 years ago; tomatoes have a quarter less calcium; Basmati rice has cheaper rice added, and sea foods as well as chicken are injected with water to increase their weight; some breads are full of emulsifiers, bleach, water and grease.

Thursday ◆ **JANUARY 31**

It was a dark and stormy night, last night, but we were not prepared to find it slipping into turmoil. Having collected Charmian from her cottage we drove to Valerie's cottage for supper. On arrival, no one greeted us. The sitting room and kitchen were deserted, although the table was laid with candles ready to be lit. Jenny called up the small stairway and discovered our hostess half way down.

"I think she's fainted!" Jenny called. Charmian handed up a glass of water and it seemed that Valerie was re-entering the conscious world. But no, not really. She remained seated staring down at us. She gave us a little wave, then Rosemary Callam and her husband arrived. Now, able to speak, Valerie indicated there was champagne in the fridge and we should open it, then extract the pheasant casserole from the oven and have supper without her. We opened the champagne and the five of us devoured it. Jenny and I peeled seven hard-boiled eggs in the kitchen and turned down the oven. It became clear that supper was off. After a brief committee meeting we agreed that we should depart, and perhaps return for supper the following evening.

The Callams left. We then turned off the lights and made our exit. For supper, we decided to forage elsewhere. "Don't worry,"

I said, "I will buy us supper in a Pub !" It was then that we admitted that neither Charmian, Jenny or myself had brought any money with us – not even a penny! No matter, we would go to The Kinneuchar Inn (where we were known) and throw ourselves upon their mercy and settle the bill tomorrow. Nay chance! The Kinneuchar management had sent the staff home as there were so few customers for food. In fact there was only one customer visible. A solitary figure at the Bar.

We decided to try The Ship Inn down at the harbour. As Jenny turned the car I entered the normally busy Bar to discover that there was no custom there – just two Barmen playing darts. "Sorry," they said. "We're closing at nine." It was just a few minutes to the hour, so we drove away, dropped Charmian at her cottage and returned home. She said she had some soup. Fortunately, we had the Vichyssoise I had made earlier.

I had just written the above when Charmian rang to say that she had been in touch with Valerie and that we were to visit her tonight when it was devoutly to be hoped the eggs and a piping hot casserole – and our hostess – would be ready.

I will remind myself to bring my wallet (just in case) this time. And a bottle of champagne.

An e-mail from Tony today gives us an up-date on Owen's condition. He is still in hospital, and will be there for some time. Apart from septicaemia and other troubles he seems to have Parkinson's Dementia, and it is this which, among other things, gives him terrible dreams and hallucinations. When Tony returns home Zac and Clare arrive for a few days from Australia, then Nicola (also from Melbourne) takes over for a week or two, to be followed by Carol from Nicosia.

Friday ◆ FEBRUARY 1

SHE SAID NO TO THE NAZIS

Last night, at 7.15 we drove round to Charmian's cottage to uplift her and proceed to Valerie's place for the supper we did not have with her last evening. We were out of luck…AGAIN! Charmian said the visit was off. I had put the promised bottle of champagne in the car, so we drove, again, to The Kinneuchar Inn. Happily, this time, the staff were on duty and we were able to drink the fizz and eat supper there.

Saturday ◆ FEBRUARY 2

Today we are to have lunch at The Wee Restaurant with Jenny's cousins up from Buckinghamshire for the Scotland v France rugby encounter. Snow is forecast. The rugby should be playable, as Murrayfield has under-pitch heating. Jim and Barbara's train was on time at Inverkeithing where we met them, and our table for five was ready. We enjoyed an excellent lunch, with wine releasing shared memories. Weatherwise we were still lucky. Blizzards had imprisoned motorists on the A66 around Brough and Bowes, and places in North Yorkshire were without electricity. Massive snowfalls in central China were reported, trapping literally millions of people.

Two of the Six Nations rugby matches will be played this afternoon: Ireland v Italy and England v Wales. When we lived in Edinburgh Jenny and I used to shake cans in the West Stand Car Park, collecting money for Trefoil House (for people with disabilities) where I sat on one of the committees. It was a good gig. We collected the dosh by working up and down the long lines of cars where boots were open and picnics in full swing. We also found lunch there, as lots of friends not only paid up but offered us smoked salmon and champagne.

Well, the Ireland - Italy match was a bit scrappy, with a close win by Ireland. England were all over Wales in the other match, but then Wales came out in the second half and with tremendous application turned the whole thing around and ended up victorious.

Sunday ◆ FEBRUARY 3

We put both dogs into the car and drove to Edinburgh, arriving at Harmony in Barnton Avenue ahead of all other guests. We had no idea who they might be, but the first to arrive after us was Anne Matheson, widow of Fr. Theseus, a headmaster of distinction. A man much loved and missed. On our return home I wrote a 'thank you' for such a splendid lunch.

"Dear Sylvia and Ian,

    BLIMEY !

    Or should we say Blighty? All the well-kent yet half-forgotten faces! Many sipping water, and some going bust on the blushful red and Marlborough White. And everyone, tucking into a Winter spread! Every dish was delish. Every cheese made to please. Salads for vitamins and napery wi' numbers. A most happy idea and I confess to enjoying quite a few ladies, while Jenny got hugs from ageing rugger buggers! You did us proud (as you always do), and it was good to find Ian moving with alacrity and grace. A Spring in his step. This is a genuine, gold-tipped thank you letter for asking us to join the party after Elie Church."

    On returning home we learned that Scotland had bit the Murrayfield dust, alas! It was sad. But, as Sylvia remarked, the game is now too dangerous. What was once a great sport has now become a business designed not so much around fitness and skill, but mainly a money spinner.

    We were two of some 25 at that Harmony party, and after drinks in the conservatory were bidden to our tables. Jenny was at a long table (*L'Aperatif*). There was also Pompadour and The Cafe Royal. (Our knives and forks were wrapped round with numbers for names so that we knew which room we had to start in). I started in the Pomp and then moved to Royal.

Monday ◆ FEBRUARY 4

Letters to write – and more letters. Then, I thought to take a look at the entry in my previous diary for February 4th. I was clearly busy with my novel Last Bus to Primrose Hill and, in part, my diary read – 'I continued planning and tried to keep hold of my six main characters who are beginning to dictate the action. Serenity Thong may disappoint me, but Jill is probably going to break my heart. Now, I need to settle the calendar, the real time in which the action takes place. It depends on Bush and Blair, We are almost in a state of war with Iraq. Meantime, we mourn with all Americans and many, many more, after the dreadful re-entry accident to Space shuttle Columbia.' (All the astronauts were burned alive).

Amid the daily avalanche of mail today there came one decent item. It is the catalogue from The Peruvian Connection. If anyone has even the slightest interest in the fashion scene, they should drool over Peruvian. How about the copywriting? (Quote about a lace skirt): – swooning in lacy tiers, our crocheted pima skirt fuses romance with craftsmanship – slim through the hip, descending past the knee to a slight A-line sweep, this piece will serve for a lifetime of celebrations.

Tuesday ◈ **FEBRUARY 5**

Shrove Tuesday. Shrovetide is also the day when we are supposed to go around singing for money. As a lad I used to have singing lessons at York Minster, but I don't think I'd merit a penny today! It is pouring with rain. Jenny is Spring cleaning the bedroom. I went to buy ham, cheese, pate, leeks, onions, sprouts and oranges. I am living a useless life and again suffering from North British Moral Moments. I have a very self-indulgent life style. Parties and pate and profiteroles. What use to man or beast is that? What's the point? feed the dogs. Put a bit of money in the charity box, but nothing seems to matter as pillows of grey cloud darken the day. Is it Black Dog again? Not in the USA, where today is the very important Tuesday as the nation stands up to be counted. Caucus time. For the Republicans it will surely be McCain for President. For the Democrats, who can say? Hillary Clinton or Obama. A lady, a Black man, a retired soldier. Which of those three will, hand on heart, pick up the pen in the Oval Office? In India and China they are probably saying "Who cares? The sun is setting in the West. It is our turn now to rule the world."

Wednesday ◈ **FEBRUARY 6**

It is obvious who is succeeding in the race to The White House. McCain, I guess, has already done the business for the Republican Party, just as Hillary Clinton will be the Democrats brightest star. The Super Tuesday result is the expected one. Obama has won more States than Clinton, but Clinton's States contain more voting power (Delegates). Short of a sudden upset, that is how it will be before my Journal ends. But will McCain beat Hillary by a short head? Whoever wins the final prize will find high office can bring you low, and at best will be a roller-coaster ride rather than a bowl of jello. An economic recession in The West could bite. And here's a conundrum: if the Democratic Party was to take power could there really be a tandem (a duo) in the White House? Nothing is certain.

Thursday ◆ **FEBRUARY 7**

This really is a dreadful month here on a wet and windy hillside. Difficult to be cheery. Also, there are repeated warnings that we are slowly slipping into a recession. Another cut in the interest rate. At home reading comes to the rescue and I have been looking at entries for February in other diaries. Boswell (in 1762) was certainly out of temper. He wrote the following to the treacherous Louisa. 'Madam: My surgeon will soon have a demand upon me of five guineas for curing the disease which you have given me. I must therefore remind you of the little sum which you had of me some time ago. You cannot have forgot upon what footing I let you have it. I neither paid it for prostitution nor gave it in charity. It was fairly borrowed, and you promised to return it. I give you notice that I expect to have it before Saturday ennight. Send the money sealed up. I have nothing more to say to you.'

The Duff Cooper Diaries (1915 - 1951) were also worth a look. For February 15th, 1922 he wrote ' Edward Cunard – nephew of Lady Cunard – has been had up for accosting private soldiers in the Park. He pleaded guilty and was fined £5. He now of course says that he was innocent and that his solicitors told him to -plead guilty in order to prevent it getting into the papers. But it has appeared in the papers all the same. Nobody talks of anything else.'

A February 18th entry in my 2003 diary reads 'A present of a small diary from Irene Fehrman, who asks me to meet her again in May at The Russell Hotel, St. Andrews. She is an amazing survivor from Nazi Germany who has spent 40 years trying to find me. She will hire a taxi to bring her from Heysham (Lancs) to

Fife. That is what she did in 2001. I first met her in Brighton and recall that she was wearing a green bikini. Now, there's a much cheerier thought on a drab Winters' day! The fact is that every year since 2001 she has come by taxi to Fife, and Jenny and I take her to lunch, or give her lunch here at home. She survived astonishing dangers and privation when she refused to join the Hitler Youth. All her friends were sent to concentration camps. She lost three husbands and her entire family, a very rich family on the borders of Germany and Poland. Her mother banked in gold bars before the Russians, driving into Germany destroyed the family estate. Irene somehow survived and became a teacher. She escaped to the West pushing her new born baby in a pram across no-man's land. I know some of the story, but not all of it, because she will not tell me everything. She still sends me post cards and I have no doubt that she will appear in Fife again later this year.

Friday ◆ FEBRUARY 8

Marriage is different in this day and age, with wives busy with their careers and, indeed, with the gym, or pool, ski slopes or golf course. Take our marriage. Jenny was off to golf this morning (a competition) and will be home in time for tea. Her golfing season, as a club committee member has begun and will last at least until October. That means she will be occupied playing and or working almost every day. Her church duties will also keep her busy through the year so that 'home' will mainly mean some gardening when weather allows, and cooking the evening meal. I am suggesting that husbands and wives, more and more, go their separate ways. This could be one – but only one – of the reasons why there now seems to be so much divorce and or other forms of separation. It is different where the marriage contains young children, and yet even then nowadays there seems to be a sad increase in the number of lone women.

Saturday ◆ FEBRUARY 9

This morning the sun is shining. It's an idle life, and I have been thinking about mistakes. The Archbishop of Canterbury has just made one. In a speech, attempting to be his usual liberal self, he strayed over into Muslim politics. At least that is how many people interpreted what he said. Among a great number of critics who took him to task were many very senior C of E Christians, including two Bishops, as well as the Media en masse, and others who shouted "Resign!" What madness. Archbishops, like any other member of the human race, must be allowed to make mistakes and be misunderstood. In a fast-changing world there will be all manner of mistakes made inside and outwith Politics, the Church, and the armed Forces. Think of Iraq and Afghanistan.

For the record both those invasions are being proven to be mistakes by a large section of Western society, and not least by France and Germany. And now Jenny has just made a mistake. She confessed "I forgot to go to The Lent course this morning!"

Fortunately we did not forget to go to Pat and Ian Haxton's house for a drink before moving up to the clubhouse. We discussed the rugby. Groans because Wales beat Scotland.

Sunday ◆ FEBRUARY 10

Last night we had the clubhouse to ourselves. I started with a tumble of prawns accompanied by small fillets of soused herring, a miniature ring of squid and a few tiny mussels. A mulled wine sorbet followed. My main course was a salmon fillet on a bed of rice with a side plate of vegetables. I finished with a plate of small artisan cheeses which I shared with Ian.

Monday ◆ FEBRUARY 11

Fog is called a Haar in Scotland. In England's North-East they often call it a Sea Fret. A grey, un-seeing situation which joints and motorists don't like. I could do with a little warmth, with the news so generally foggy. I suspect BBC and Sky editors are offering news as entertainment. How else can we, the proles and pebbledash people view it? Do we care that McCartney's Bank account amounts to at least £800 millions and that his legal settlement with the one-legged Mills will be heard in camera?

Today, I will buy Valentine Cards and try to remember to say my prayers as Jenny goes out to play bridge.

Tuesday ◆ FEBRUARY 12

This morning I have started enquiries from builders with a view to having the conservatory put into tough weather order. The brick base and tiled floor are as good as new, but the timber that was used for the upper section, including windows and roof is rotting from the inside.

This afternoon – an early lunch, then off to The Corn Exchange in Cupar to attend a NADFAS illustrated talk on Matisse by a Mr. Frank Woodgate who is a lecturer and guide at Tate Modern. As ever, the Blue Rinse Ladies turned out in their hundreds, eagerly awaiting their monthly bite of culture, but alas! No Mr. Woodgate. He was still grounded at London City Airport on account of fog. So the Ladies managed to get an authority on antique furniture, an educated man who gave a lecture on Dumfries House which has recently been purchased from the Marquis of Bute by a consortium including Historic Scotland. The cost (of the house) was £45 million. It was built by the Adam brothers and the furniture it contains, said the lecturer, "is worth more than the house." As for our auld hoose and injured conservatory, I have asked a Mr. Thain, a builder, to call in tomorrow to see if he might give us a quote for a re-build. We had a look at the conservatory his lads recently completed for the Cowan's on the hilltop, and we liked the workmanship.

Wednesday ◆ FEBRUARY 13

Mr. Thain called in this afternoon and we gave him tea in the conservatory, plus some written instructions with a view to a re-build. He turned out to be very tall with an agreeable manner and an ability to talk non-stop. We had a very thorough discussion and he took a couple of photographs of the outside of the conservatory. He left saying that he would get back to us with a plan and estimates very soon.

Thursday ◆ FEBRUARY 14

St Valentine's Day. Millions of pounds will have been spent on cards, candles, roses, champagne, chocolate and candlelight suppers. All for love...on one day. Why can't we have love every day. The great pot of money might have been better spent on improved pensions for the aged, better schools, or subsidies to keep costs of food, heating and lighting from going through the roof. Or even use the money to provide extra, and much-needed aid to under-developed countries attempting to grow in the face of the big, greedy world economies. I bought Jenny a Valentine card, she bought me one, and I sent two to the girls in the Pharmacy including a double ticket to Paradise, Business Class (for Susan and me, of course!).

Nancy rang from York to say that Owen did not have the operation after all. I am desperately sorry for him. He is a stoic and brave. For me, when worry/anxiety strikes the best recipe is to DO SOMETHING. So yesterday I made some soup for today. I must now reply to more invitations and also consider reserving tickets to some concerts in the Summer East Neuk Festival which is becoming a national treasure, lauded by all the critics. For tickets at £10 a head we get Beethoven, Mendelssohn, Bach, Smetana, Schubert, Janacek, and modern composers with fine artistes performing. How about medieval choral music, by candlelight in St. Monans Kirk.

I notice that The Old Reekie Band's gig is named in the programme on the night after the candlelight choral concert. We will play for dancing in Kinkell Byre from 9.00 p.m. Tickets £10 per person.

Friday ◆ FEBRUARY 15

I delivered an Auld Reekie CD to Grey Eyes in South Street. She and husband Jim are my most favourite people living here by the sea, just as they were in Edinburgh. At the door they said something I have not heard for years; "Will you not come in and sit for a while?" A charming invitation. However, I was on my way to buy a steak at The Farm Shop and purchase milk, bananas and eggs. And there you go! Should I feel guilty, all this luxury when there are thousands who can afford so little. Even in Britain there are children who are not getting enough to eat.

Saturday ◆ FEBRUARY 16

Jenny went off to her Lenten course. On returning she reported that the Minister Brian had remarked to Elaine that Jenny was fortunate to be married to a Quaker because there would be Peace. He added, with a wink, that Jenny could therefore always do as she wished. Yeah – she does! Later we bought some venison and wild boar sausages for supper. Apart from that, this was a bit of a nothing day. Before supper I decided to make an old fashioned cocktail. The Balalika consists of two parts vodka, two parts cointreau with lemon juice, shaken (not stirred) over ice.

Sunday ◆ FEBRUARY 17

Off to Meeting in St. Andrews. Jenny came with me, not to Meeting but to do some shopping in the supermarket. Two Friends ministered at Meeting to a gathering of about 20. Over coffee afterwards we were asked to contribute to a medical charity serving asylum seekers. I wished we did not have so many asylum seekers, but when you think of the way the world is we are ALL in the asylum.

We had an unexpected phone call from Sandy and Grizelda Cowan who live on the hilltop behind us. They had heard we took a peep at their new conservatory so asked us to come and take a proper look. The house was also new, built about two years ago, modern but not particularly handsome, until you enter. The interior is excellently planned. A luxurious nest that demonstrated what you can do if you have some serious money to spend. The conservatory to the rear of the house is a quality feature with under-floor heating.

Monday ◆ FEBRUARY 18

Jenny to the Golf House Club this morning, and to Bridge at Jean Begg's this afternoon. It is not easy writing this journal with two dogs careering around the house and barking fit to bust!

The Northern Rock nonsense continues. Nationalisation is the short term rescue plan with a new Chief Exec. to steer the early stages. The Government is now the shareholder. Is the country fast slipping down the tubes? We are an ill-governed, selfish, failing Democracy, but at least we have freedom of speech and a free Press and Media. Not that the editors of this valuable commodity give much cheer. How long, oh Lord, will they continue to serve up the continuing rubbish over Princess Di's decease and 'murder' plot. How much longer must the Madeleine McCann epic run? Meantime there is bad news from Iraq, Afghanistan and not least from Pakistan where a corrupt election is about to take place.

Tuesday ◆ FEBRUARY 19

Among the phone calls today was one from Marcia Ritchie. Did we want to go to a performance of Romeo and Juliet by Dundee Rep. Yes of course we did. We are keen supporters of the Rep and the four of us will go as usual (next month) and have supper first in the theatre's café. There was a succession of nonsense calls, but a serious one from York. Owen seems to be a little improved. Maybe he will be able to leave hospital quite soon.

Wednesday ◆ FEBRUARY 20

An e mail giving a quotation for the re-build of the conservatory arrived today. The company called Finesse gives us several options. After considerable thought we prefer what the boss, Neil Thain, styles as Option 2. This allows for an all-mahogany structure above our existing brick base, with a slate roof. The conservatory is so sited as to welcome any sunlight literally from dawn to dusk and even with windows and doors wide open it becomes incredibly hot – hence our expensive blinds, made to measure and fitted. Option 2 is costed at £16,000 complete and insured for 10 years.

Today is Charity Day. Jenny has gone to her Pilates class while I have started sorting out shirts I never seem to wear and which will go to a charity shops in St. Andrews. I have selected

12 shirts (which have hardly been worn) and some trousers. This leaves me a bit short on trousers but still with at least 18 nearly new shirts, and six more still in their packages, unworn. I reckon I could get by with a total of 7 shirts, not counting evening (black tie shirts).

Alison Chapman, up from Sussex, came for lunch and we had a big jaw-jaw. Entertaining her is a pleasure and always easy because she likes to laugh a lot.

Thursday ◆ FEBRUARY 21

Very cold. High wind. House draughty. Millie prowled half the night, frightened of the gale, and spent the other half on our bed. Gemma started crying in her cage until we released her. At Jenny's command I wrote a card to Clare Dickson (in Wimbledon). Her first born is called Isla and apparently has black hair. Jenny remembers everyone's birth. And death. She is off to a funeral today followed by drinks in the Club. Then to Church affairs. Yes, we ARE the chattering classes – or Pebbledash people. But, hooray! Two MPs have at last complained publicly about the continuing nonsense, and waste of money, on the legal farce concerning Princess Diana's death years ago. The wind is fingering the slates on the roof. Do your worst! "Blow, winds, and crack your cheeks! rage! blow! You cataracts and hurricanoes spout Till you have drench'd our steeples, drown'd the cocks!" (etcetera).

This afternoon I sat with the dogs who were clearly upset by the gale. They cuddled close. We shared chairs while I read a glossy brochure which was posted to us from Quinta do Lago, presumably because of our ownership in the club there. The brochure was of academic interest only. It came from "The European Real Estate Network" (EREN) and featured their international property symposium held in Valencia. It pictured, and offered, beautiful properties in Austria, Denmark, Germany, Greece, Ireland, Italy, Spain, Portugal, Switzerland, Dubai, the Caribbean, and the USA. In Dubai "the real estate market is one of the strongest and most dynamic in the world with annual price increases of at least 15 - 20 per cent. and a population that is growing at the rate of approx 700 new residents per day all the year round." Ye Gods! Prices mainly range from £1 million to around £15 million.

Friday ◈ FEBRUARY 22

Birthday. Ushered in this morning by a 60 or 70 mph gale battering the cottage. Cards at breakfast time, and at least four of them had wine or food as a theme. Even as I write another card arrives which announces Vino, pizza, spaghetti, olives, and pasta! The dogs were quiet. Too quiet. Jenny had gone up to the farm shop and I was in the bath. On emerging I discovered that Gemma had un-made the bed, found Jenny's nightdress and torn it to bits. Presently we are driving over to The Peat Inn. Jenny has kindly said she will buy me a birthday lunch there. I said I would do the wine. There was a list of 400, including vintage Krug at £240 a bottle. We had not visited The Peat Inn since Wilson left. The new management has style and probably deserves a Michelin. Sofas in the small entrance lounge. The huge fireplace with burning logs. Two lovers holding hands and drinking gin.

We were shown to a table in the first of several dining areas. and given small warm loaves (six different flavours) and a minute bowl containing a warm broth of sweet potato, carrots and aniseed. To start we both chose Smoked Haddock Veloute with soft poached quails eggs. The broth was delicious. For mains Jenny selected Roast fillet of Pork with braised red cabbage, walnuts, bacon and Juniper jus. I chose Plaice Meuniere with ratte potatoes and beurre noisette. For pud Jenny had the Creme Brule while I abstained and took black coffee instead. We were leisurely and lazy. Back home there were more cards and a few phone calls. Watching match play golf from Arizona on TV I learned that Vijay Singh was also having a birthday. Others who shared my day and month dates were George Washington, and Chopin.

Saturday ◈ FEBRUARY 23

To the Golf House Club for supper which Geoffrey and Vivi Millar arranged. With us were Colin and Elaine Ross, and Murray and Dorothy Stewart. There was only one other table occupied. It was organised by Elizabeth and David Simpson. Half way through our meal we learned with a dreadful shock, and disbelief, that Gavin and Margot Anderson who should have been at the second table had not appeared. Earlier in the day – around about lunchtime – it seemed that Margot had collapsed on the staircase of her home here, and was unconscious. She was promptly taken to hospital where a cerebral haemorrhage was diagnosed. The condition is un-operable and it is feared that she is 'brain dead.' It happened without warning. I can understand this. My youngest brother Robin, when aged eight, went to bed in the nursery a happy, fit child. Several hours later he died from the same illness in his mother's arms.

It was little more than a month ago that Jenny and I stayed with Gavin and Margot in Edinburgh, They were both in fine form, and Margot was managing very well with a plaster on her left ankle which she had broken – again at the foot of the stair in their seaside home. She had also just had a cataract in one eye treated.

We are all sorely hit, and not least by other disasters here. Euan Colquhon is a survivor of a stroke, but has no speech and cannot walk. Michael Barratt recently also suffered a stroke and is in a wheelchair for ever. David Cowan fell on the 17th hole at Muirfield and is similarly disabled, with no movement in two arms and legs, while Sandra McCabbe is trying to recover from a stroke. All this plus two funerals the other day.

Euan was a fine golfer – very active, noisy, cheerful and a great host. Michael is a retired Headmaster of Loch Rannoch, and again was a very fit man. David had very recently retired from a career as a popular Edinburgh consultant surgeon, and a much admired golfer, and Sandra is a cheery wee bundle, and wife of Tom whom she helps as ship's chandler here.

And there's more. I was recently in touch with Alec Beveridge who lent me a book he was given by Curtis Strange, former American Ryder Cup captain. Alec (St. Andrews Links Trust) is grounded with Parkinsons, like my brother. Then, of course, there is good neighbour and friend Jean Glen and her husband Alan, former Perthshire farmer, golfer and international

Curling champion, and he is unwell. I worry for friends we all love and admire, and I have been astonished that these disasters happen to mortals who were especially active, and physically fit. All this, and in a place that is considered to be one of the healthiest playgrounds in the UK.

Sunday ◆ FEBRUARY 24

Jenny went to her church, and I drove over to St. Andrews. Quaker Meeting was smaller than usual. Several Friends ministered, but two of them mumbled so quietly that I could not understand what they were attempting to say. After the meeting for worship there was to be a kind of Arab lunch in sympathy with the Palestinian people whose lands had been occupied illegally by Israel. I did not stay. I needed some escapism, so returned home to TV. I noted that in The Six Nations Wales is heading for victory and that England defeated the sexy French.

Monday ◆ FEBRUARY 25

This morning we sent an e-mail to Neil Thain telling him to go ahead with the conservatory re-build. He won't make a start for a while. It is wickedly cold outside.

Oh my God! What next? I have just heard that Tom Meldrum is now in hospital with "a heart attack." He is the big man, a strong man, with a busy gardening business.

So what do you do in a time of waiting ? Read the Sunday Times mags, Culture and Style. The latter is for women of course, but I scan it for the daft prose style used by their regular writers which gets more extreme by the week.

Tuesday ◆ FEBRUARY 26

Outside the gale must be 60 or 70 mph. I could hardly stand up against it as it sweeps across the golf course to batter our exposed cottage It clearly howls into a grill or waste pipe on the West-facing wall and causes a rhythmical rumpus in the bathroom, an unending bump, bump, bump. I attempted to block the grill outside but it made no difference so I rang Peattie the plumber. Later I had an inspiration: I un-plugged and ran the bath tap briefly. Eureka! The thumping ceased.

Wednesday ◈ FEBRUARY 27

From dawn a low but blinding sun. It cheered us up – maybe Spring is on the way. Jenny off to the club, then to her Pilates class. I was hit by a filthy, sudden cold in the head, so I rested, then we drove to St. Andrews for an early supper in L'Orient, the Thai and Japanese restaurant. There is nothing to compare with a really hot green chicken curry for clearing the sinus.

Thursday ◈ FEBRUARY 28

I now feel utterly wasted, having just written to Gavin about Margot. There is little or no change in her condition apparently, and even if she does regain consciousness it seems that she will have no speech. And, as if this was not bad enough, it appears that David Cowan has suffered a second stroke. Here by the sea there is a dreadful cloud hovering. Families and friends are having such hurt. I have just sent David's sister Anne her birthday card – there is to be a celebration for her in the club. What are we celebrating but mortality.

Jenny played another golf tie today. She and Suzie beat Hilary and Liz Childs. I did more shopping, then made soup and the sardine pate like the one which, not long ago, I took to David when he was chair-bound.

Friday ◈ FEBRUARY 29

An e mail from Anthony in Melbourne informs us that Owen is now back home and doing well. Nicky is still there and organising home helps. It is therefore time that we went down to York to visit, so I have booked a night at Four Gables in Boston Spa. We will stay one night there, then hope to get a bed the following night on our way home at Hilltop, Newsham, with Christina.

Last night Jenny said there was a man who had called by and wanted to speak with me. I told her to tell him to come through (I had gone to bed early). I had never met him before. He was handsome and well dressed and in a rather un-mannerly way he perched on the side of the bed, then shook my hand. He explained that he wanted a word. Would I kindly give him my credit cards and Bank cards.

Incredible fellow ! I said certainly not. So, what about my wife's cards – could he have them instead? How mad can people be! I said thank you, but no, and would he please leave. I had no idea who he might be. On hearing this he pulled a small revolver from his pocket.

"You will have heard what happens in Northern Ireland," he said. "Knee caps. They shoot them and render the recipient lame. I would rather that this did not happen to you!"

I said "Stop talking rubbish. I insist you leave !" His revolver was obviously just a toy. This was some kind of game. I was, however, wrong. He took aim and fired at the dressing table mirror, which shattered. I was furious and alarmed. I reached for the bedside phone. "I'll get the Police" "I don't think you will," he replied. "The lines are down. I have seen to that."

"For God's sake, Jenny !" I shouted, "Get the car…NO, better go get David next door!"

"I don't think she will," the man said. "I have seen to him as well!" At that point, I woke up, sweating. It was not as pleasant as the dream I had the previous night. She was astonishingly beautiful. I passionately desired her, but was refused. Years later I saw her again. She was seated before her mirror and filing her nails. I tip-toed across to her and tapped on her knee with one finger. She turned. Oh! that beatific smile. Who was she?

She said "I'm married."

I can recall most of my dreams. Hardly had I typed that last word when the phone rang. It was Ian Ritchie asking if I would speak a word of thanks to Hilary (Captain of the Ladies Golf Club) and to himself and to Stuart Hutton at the Mixed Dinner of Seniors and their wives. I am no speech-maker, but I have had to say yes.

Ian then told me that David Cowan died last night. Jenny is upset. In a sense it is better that he has not had to live on, speechless, and unable to use arms or legs. But Jenny and David grew up together. She said "He was like a Brother to me."

Saturday ◈ MARCH 1

ROMEO, JULIET — AND OBAMA

Jenny cooked a beautiful supper last night. David arrived bearing gifts. A bottle of Merlot for me, and a gardening apron for Jenny. We settled to drinks and some sardine pate I had made. Mushroom soup (which I had also made) was followed by Fillet steak, peas, carrots, new potatoes, then Christmas pudding with brandy (and custard), cheese and biscuits. The next course was a discussion on Faith and I explained my high wire attempts, I keep falling off the high wire. losing Faith then climbing back on again. David and Jenny, as Elders of the Kirk, are more balanced and never seem to fall off.

Thinking of faith, I received a letter from faithful Irene, the lady who each year drives all the way from Heysham in a taxi to see me, as well as writing greetings. This greeting, written on February 28th read as follows: 'Dear Michael, you had a nice birthday. The main thing is, you are well. Chopin is my favourite composer. Thank you so much for your card. I treasure the drawings. Now I am reading another book, Where the Rainbow Ends. The weather is gorgeous. I rejoice in the garden. After snowdrops now crocus and daffodils. Morecambe gets better and better. I saw a pantomime. Snow White and the Seven Dwarfs. I never stop whistling. Greetings to Jenny. One cactus is in full bloom in the library. Love from Irene'.

She is an amazing survivor of Nazi Germany who turned her back on Hitler and his Gestapo and now will not think or speak of the homeland she has totally renounced in favour of living in Lancashire.

Sunday ◈ MARCH 2

Mothering Sunday. Prince Harry, third in line to the Throne, has returned from Afghanistan and is called "the Warrior Prince, and a hero." He will never see his mother. To his credit he denies being a hero and longs to return to the war to kill or be killed. I see no sense in that. Nor do I see any sense in a British Army being in that country. It is simply another killing field, as is Gaza now, with a lot of civilians being slaughtered by Israel. Killing of women and children in war has for some years now been conveniently called "collateral damage." Anyway, as it seems to be Mothers' Day I thought I should buy Jenny something. So I purchased green grapes, bread and a dozen red roses.

Monday ◆ MARCH 3

Drove to Edinburgh. We planned to look for garden furniture but the two stores we tried said we were too early and the chairs and table we sought would not be in stock for several weeks. The next call was to Candlemaker Row where I would attend the Monks of St. Giles' March Chapter while Jenny made her periodic visit to M&S. We were early, with an hour on our hands, so repaired to The New Club for tea.

The Chapter, with Prior's Nips prompt at 7.00 p.m., was thinner than usual, with Fr. Pillius deputising for Prior Botulus who had disappeared to New Zealand. Fr. Calamus (Sir. William Reid) deputised for the Fiscal Aquila (Gavin Anderson) whose wife Margot is still in a coma. It is a dreadful waiting time.We had refection, and I had excellent conversation with Pullarius and Penurius. After the Fiscals rosta the Light was passed to the Prior and I was first to read my verse ('That Extra Mile') as I had to leave by 9.00 p.m. when Jenny arrived to collect me. Gemma and Millie were in the car. We had brought them to town and we did not want their confinement to be too long.

Tuesday ◆ MARCH 4

My tongue discovered a broken, or chipped, tooth. I attempted to ring Peter Davidson (dental surgeon) but he is at the dental hospital in Dundee all today. I then had to go to the surgery and get my INR. The beautiful, the beatific Clare Francis said the results of the blood tests I had done were all clear, but agreed that there was nothing much to be done about arthritis or my injured joints.

Back home the phone seemed to ring non stop. Someone wanted to sell our time share in Quinta; mechanic Bob wanted to call to fit a new wing mirror; Judy Mason wanted Ann Riddle's address, then – David with sad news. The lovely Jay Dowling, whose wife Rosie died (cancer) about a year ago, died last Friday (more cancer). The funeral will be in Hillsborough.

Jenny had left a note advising me to ring Suzy Delaney for an appointment. She was unavailable but rang back later. Jenny had left to play another golf tie. She returned with news that she and her partner had again been successful.

Charmian, and Carolyn (from Guernsey) arrived. Carolyn had come over for a funeral. It seems to be a dark, dark time for us all. The one bright spot was an invitation to a wedding in St. Andrews. Fraser McQuarrie is to marry his girl, a bright young doctor.

I feel sore about Jay Dowling. He and Rosie were Portugal friends, for that is where we first met them. We were sitting in the Club lounge, both waiting to drive to the airport to catch our flights home after another sunny holiday. The TV was showing golf which reminded Jay (whom we had not met before) that the British Open would be in St. Andrews in July, We chatted and he said he had hoped to get over from Ireland to the Old Course. But, he added, "Unhappily, Graeme and Jenny Simmers have a house full and so we have not anywhere to stay." I replied "Yes, you have, you can come and stay with us, we are just 20 minutes from St. Andrews." Jay replied that they couldn't possibly take such a liberty. Rosie said "Yes we can – thank you, we'd love to!" And that is how our friendship began. In subsequent years, every Monday morning in Portugal it was "Brandy and a tart!" on a pavement café in Loule as together we planned a round of golf. Rosie played off 2 and Jay was 8 or 9.

Wednesday ◆ MARCH 5

Peter Davidson repaired the tooth and we attended to 'shopping'. To Boots, to Rodgers for cinnamon, and to the silver shop. Here I left my old Rolex watch for cleaning, while Jenny showed her

Aunts gold wristwatch for valuation. The shop said the pure gold strap would be valuable and that Jenny should take it to Sotherby's in Edinburgh. We drove home for an early lunch, then Jenny departed for Craigihill near Perth for a handicap seminar. On returning she will grab a boiled egg before attending a Church meeting in the village. It's a non-stop life.

News from across The Pond. McCain has clearly won the Republican nomination for President. It is now less certain who will do battle in November for the Democrats. Hillary Clinton has just won three out of four important Primaries and is thus catching up Obama. It's a neck- and-neck life.

Joyous news closer to home. Mark and Verity have added to their young family with 'Jamie, born March 3rd and weighing in at 8 lbs. It's a fecund life! After my tooth treatment Peter Davidson asked whether The Auld Reekie Dance Band could supply music for St. Andrews' Rotary Club Garden Party. Some 330 Rotarians would attend on Sunday June 15th at Airdrie House, near Anstruther. I promised I would give him an answer as soon as I had checked with Rachel.

Thursday ◈ MARCH 6

Jenny was due to play another tie this morning, but the wind was so strong and cold the match was called off. Tonight she will come with me to the Golf House Club to attend the Seniors' Mixed Dinner party – some 40 Seniors with their wives, or someone else's wife. Black tie. I have to do a vote of thanks (as Ian had commanded).

Telephones. e-mails. Letters. The Band is unable to do the Rotary Club gig. Rachel will be in St. Petersburg on June 15th. Peter Gordon will be rehearsing on the Sunday afternoon in question, and MacMillan is likely to be in France. So I will have to disappoint the dentist. I have asked Ray Elrick if his Band could oblige.

The good news is that Rachel's daughter Holly is to marry Manolo (from Granada) in August and the Auld Reekie Band is to play for the dancing.

Friday ◆ MARCH 7

We took the dogs to the kennels on the hill then drove to Edinburgh for the funeral of David Cowan in St. Cuthberts at the West End, (the church in which Jenny and I were married). At least 400 attended the funeral. The pews and gallery were crowded with the medical/surgical profession, with Edinburgh and Fife friends, with golfers from Muirfield and the R & A and other clubs, including The Pirates, and of course those with whom he worked at The Sick Kids Hospital. Professor Bertie Wood, a lifelong friend, spoke excellently, as did David's eldest son Chris. Afterwards we walked over to the Caledonian Hotel to drink wine and eat a sandwich lunch with many friends we had not seen for months, even years. It was astonishing to see David's mother, Meryl, at the Service. She had been driven over from the coast in a private ambulance. I think she is 96.

Later we drove to Kilmaurs Terrace to have tea with Chico and Kathy, followed by an early supper. I took wine, and some provisions from Victor Hugo in The Meadows including sun dried tomatoes, black olives and two interesting cheeses.

Saturday ◆ MARCH 8

We collected the dogs from Arncroach. Driving home a rain squall almost brought us to a standstill. Flash floods. It is the Calcutta Cup this afternoon. The talented Welsh pack won the Triple Crown, but England were thrashed by Scotland who played brilliantly in the most atrocious conditions.

Sunday ◆ MARCH 9

I took Jenny and Mrs Grey to Church then drove on to Anstruther to pick up Rosina and attend Meeting. About 24 of us sat quietly together for an hour. At the close Pam read her notices, while Robin announced a charity cycle run to Paris in which he was to take part. Back home Bob the mechanic returned the blue car after repairing mirror and brakes.

Monday ◆ MARCH 10

More letters to write, with a thank you to the Fraser family for their invitation to the marriage of daughter Emily to F. McQuarrie next month at St. Salvator's in St. Andrews. This morning Jenny to Pilates, and then Bridge at Joy Young's house.

Bonham's rang to say the gold watch we left with them is valued at £400 to £600. They would put it in the relevant Sale in July. Gold has gone up steeply in price.

The wars in Iraq and Afghanistan are costing a cool £3 $\frac{1}{4}$ BILLON. Costs in Iraq have risen by 122 per cent and over 70 per cent in Afghanistan.

Weather: In soggy England there are 41 flood warnings. Winds 80 mph. Bridges closed. 7,000 homes without power. Road, rail and air traffic severely affected.

Tuesday ◆ MARCH 11

Today, blinding sun and blue skies. We raced over to Buckhaven with Millie. There she will get her coat cut for the Summer. Then Jenny went off to her copying of accounts for the church. Gemma attacked the coriander, scattered leaves on the floor and then brought the empty pack to show me how clever she had been.

Tomorrow we drive to York to see Owen. Gemma and Millie will go to kennels for a couple of nights. There is more sadness. The popular Chief Constable of Greater Manchester has been found dead in high hills. Early suggestions indicate suicide. Personal notes to his family were found on his body.

Wednesday ◆ MARCH 12

We delivered the dogs to Kennels at Arncroach, then returned to pack the car and leave, at 11.00 a.m. for York. Approaching the Forth Bridge illuminated signs told us it was closed. This meant we had to cross the Forth at Kincardine Bridge 13 $\frac{1}{2}$ miles up river. Needless to say, the traffic was not only heavy, it was mostly stationary. It took us two hours to cover 13 miles, while at Kincardine there was more chaos as new road works were in hand. We eventually made it back to the Edinburgh by-pass, and after more road works and delays we arrived at Carfraemill where we stopped for a quick slurp of soup, and after three and a half hours of driving I handed over to Jenny. Heavy lorries en route, more road works and a very slow crawl round Newcastle. Then between Durham and Bishops Auckland we came to a standstill followed by two more road works hold ups. Our destination was Four Gables (a B&B) in Boston Spa just East of Wetherby. We arrived at 7.30 p.m., ie: 8 $^1/_2$ hours after leaving home! We could have flown to NEW York in half the time.

Four Gables is an Arts and Crafts house, well maintained by David and Ann Watts. The best of the several bedrooms en suite was quiet, and comfortable (It is the third time we have stayed here.)

Thursday ◆ **MARCH 13**

We appeared to be the only guests for breakfast. I chose "The full English" with one egg easy over. We were not to see Owen, now home in Fulford, until about 12 noon, so used an hour or so in the nearby Retail Outlet where Jenny bought a handsome navy evening skirt and two casual shirts.

Owen had managed to vacate his bed and was seated in the living room watched over by Nancy, and Nicola Jane from Melbourne. He looked much better than I had expected. Frail, of course, with a whisper for a voice. But he took some wine and a sandwich for lunch (we had taken him some smoked salmon). He showed me his wrists and lower arms which were covered in black scabs. He said they had been caused by the rough handling of nurses when he was in hospital. Their nails had scratched him and the wounds, earlier, had been bandaged to staunch the bleeding. I thought this unforgivable. Even worse, while he should have had a home visit from a GP none was forthcoming, and he was informed he would have to wait a fortnight before a doctor would call in. Their local surgery is no more than 100 yards from their front door. What on earth is this sector of the NHS doing? During Owen's seven weeks in hospital he had very nearly died.

We spent three hours with him before we had to leave and Owen returned to his bed. Nancy is exhausted.

We then drove up the A1 M to Scotch Corner and on to Hilltop where we checked in for the night. It is a favourite B&B kept by Christina Farmer, widow of a high ranking soldier who, after the Second World War, took charge of The Chelsea Pensioners Hospital. It was great to see Christina again, we have stayed at Hilltop several times. It is a handsome Georgian house beautifully furnished, with a sitting room that is a joy and a fine dining room. Framed pictures show Guardsman (Horse Guards?), and ladies in the saddle hunting. There are books, decanters and silverware galore. On arrival at Hilltop, as ever we were seated in front of a warm fire and brought tea, cakes and biscuits. There are only two guest rooms. Ours is up a short flight of stairs behind a latched door which leads to a bedroom and bathroom. Windows give views of the garden and a meadow in which Christina keeps two black sheep, four pheasants and a hen. We ate supper at The Travellers Rest in the nearby village of Dalton. It is a pleasant Pub with a cheerful fire in the Bar and a friendly Lab called Biscuit.

Friday ◈ MARCH 14

A Hilltop breakfast is, as the French would say, "Les Pieds!" The best! On the dining table we found 13 different packets of cereals, with nuts and seeds. Blood red grapefruit was at both our place settings. There was fresh orange juice, muesli, yoghurt, and a positive platoon of preserves, including home-made marmalade and jam, and honey and upside down Marmite. There was toast and soft bread in a basket snuggling beneath snowy linen, and a cafatiere of strong coffee. And all this was available before sausages, crispy bacon, tomatoes, mushrooms, eggs easy-over as you wish and fried bread.

Suitably refreshed, we packed, jumped into the car and then I drove like hell through the English Borders to come to a halt at The Collingwood Arms at Cornhill near Coldstream where we always used to stop for a swift half. It is under new management and has been transformed into a smart fisherman's hostelry. It was named after Vice-Admiral Collingwood who served under Nelson at Trafalgar. The Forth Bridge was open. We were home in time for tea.

Saturday ◆ MARCH 15

This morning we went to the Town Hall to see an exhibition consisting of photographs, drawings and text concerning Elie Harbour. The show was in conjunction with a book signing by Archie Rennie, retired civil servant and a former Monk of St Giles (known as Fr. Pluvius). His book is called 'The Harbours of Elie Bay.' A History. It is meticulously researched and illustrated with photographs and ancient maps. Archie signed a book for me, and later after an introduction by Graeme Meacher (Postmaster) he talked a little about his book.

After lunch came the final matches in The Six Nations. England regained a little glory by narrowly defeating Ireland; Rome echoed with joy as the Italians beat Scotland; and what everyone wanted to happen happened. Wales beat France and thus won the Grand Slam.

Sunday ◆ MARCH 16

I will enjoy 'The Harbours of Elie Bay.' The flyer reads thus: 'This is the story of Elie bay from prehistoric times until 1975, in the context of national events and movements. Picts, Romans, Northumbrians, pilgrims, medieval aristocrats, warriors, prelates, traders, merchant skippers, privateers, Cromwellian soldiers, Jacobite rebels, wealthy lairds, bankrupt lairds, religious and political refugees, exporters of coal and iron ore, smugglers, fishermen, Victorian industrialists, farmers and merchants, fugitives from justice all used the harbours of the bay. 'It continues: 'The elopement in about 1680 of a laird's daughter disguised as a swan confined in a barrel, aboard the Royal yacht of James Duke of York, governor of Scotland for his brother Charles 11, is one of the stories told here. An account of the voyages of an Elie merchant skipper of that period. He made 65 voyages in 24 years, mainly to continental ports from Norway to Bordeaux.

Jenny went off to the kirk where she had to read a Lesson from the Old Testament. We rehearsed a longish passage. I then drove over to Meeting with Rosina.

On Wednesday we are to visit Dundee Rep where 'Romeo and Juliet' is the play to be performed by the now famous ensemble. As usual, we will go with Ian and Marcia Ritchie, and this time Colin and Elaine Ross will come too. To prepare for what I think will be a treat I read some of the text. I would have liked to play the part of Mercutio. Well, why not? At Uni I was cast as Hamlet in that other tragedy, but tragically I never actually played it. The lady producer had a nervous breakdown during rehearsals! (Probably just as well). Actually, I was disappointed. I always wanted to be an actor, and in fact once went back stage to ask the great Laurence Olivier how to make a start. From his dressing room he called "Come in, dear boy!" However, I did not get much joy, he was preoccupied and still in character having just come off from playing Ibsen's Master Builder and was also unexpectedly excited: "I am dining with the Guards tonight, dear boy!"

I had to wait until I co-wrote, directed and played in an Edinburgh Festival Fringe revue. It was called 'Just the Ticket.' We had 40 rehearsals. There was music (seven piece band) and mayhem for a fortnight. In one number four of us in black robes and wearing long white beards sang one of my bits of nonsense: -

John Knox had a very sharp nose,
Well, sharp as noses goes -
But what did he do for a hanky
With a cold, do you suppose?
For the kirk it had no Kleenex
No Handy Andies too - SO
What did knicky knacky Knox's nose
Do if it needed blew?

There was more of course. A lot more. Two members of my cast got married after the show. Another one was divorced, and one was never sober!

Monday ◆ **MARCH 17**

According to my last diary, five years ago the Iraq war was about to begin with heavy bombing on Baghdad. In Edinburgh we were busy clearing the flat in St, Bernard's Crescent. Fourteen couples had a look at it (it sold quickly for more than £257,192). Real Money. How about Paul McCarthy divorce settlement. Today it was announced that Heather Mills will receive £24.3 million from Sr. Paul who wanted her to have only about £15 million. She had asked for £125 million. What rubbish.

Tuesday ◆ **MARCH 18**

Jenny out to play another tie. I cleared masses of paper, most of it junk mail. Then I spent some time reading 'The Harbours of Elie Bay.' I found it curiously appealing, my imagination tickled by the stories of pilgrims who sailed from the North Berwick coast to land at Chapel Green en route to their religious devotions in St. Andrews. Spending time, year after year, in Little Elie Mother's Chapel Green House, I little thought then that I slept and ate where those medieval pilgrims had rested after a breezy crossing of the Forth.

I endured a lengthy phone call with our insurance company concerning the signet ring I lost and wish to replace. They have agreed that if I can find a suitable ring (at Goodwin's, Edinburgh), I should have it valued and send the figure to them.

Wednesday ◆ **MARCH 19**

This evening to Romeo and Juliet. I have one quarrel with Shakespeare. Mercutio says to Romeo, who is bored with his chum's chattering, "I talk of dreams; Which are the children of an idle brain, Begot of nothing but vain fantasy." Wrong, sir! Dreams are as much a part of us as breathing. When we sleep our brains do not die, the thinking and image process continues giving us fear, delight, anxiety, even comfort, in stories and scenarios no less real than those in waking life. Not everyone remembers their dreams, but, like me, many people do. Psychotherapists live on others dreams. Last night I dreamed of money in a playlet indicating I had not sufficient money for some purpose or other.

Thursday ◆ **MARCH 20**

Alas, last night!

> 'Never was a story of more woe
> Than this of Juliet and her Romeo.'

And never was an evening of more woe than the production of the play by our much loved and admired Dundee Rep ensemble. Hope and expectation was high as the six of us ate our supper in the theatre café. But then, and then. There were some good cameo performances from several of the players, notably Ann Louise Ross (Nurse) and Cliff Burnett (Friar Lawrence). Both Romeo and Juliet worked very hard (Kevin Lennon and Hannah Donaldson), as did Mercutio (Paul Hickey). The setting, with the big bed of love descending and ascending, was in keeping with the tragic theme, and the lighting plot was excellent. But, why oh why was almost every character literally yelling at the audience from start to finish. Barely a breath was taken as words and lines that had not been chopped became hopelessly lost. Passion does not need to be so loud. Think of the grace, the tenderness, the longing in West Side Story - the lovers who sang "There's a place for us, a time and space for us, hold my hand and I'll take you there" (etc). The balcony scene was excellently devised, but here was a Romeo and a Juliet shouting their heads off, and that was plain stupid. Their billing and coo-ing could have been heard on the far side of the River Tay! There surely should have been some contrast, some hills and valleys, so that the spoken verse had more than one 'colour.'

Friday ◆ **MARCH 21**

It is Good Friday already. If "Good" – why? In Christian liturgy Jesus was crucified on Good Friday. Not good, until you are informed that in this context Good means Holy. He had to be crucified so that he could rise again. And the resurrection occurred on the third day after His crucifixion (AD 33). Minister Brian will be busy about his devotions, caring for the congregations of his three churches.

Jenny has decreed there shall be Easter Eggs. Thus, she has bought one for her nephew Peter, one for her sister Charmian – and one for us.

Five years ago my diary entry for March 20th noted that the war In Iraq had 'officially' begun. But, why are there Rules of War? In the Services you have to kill or be killed. I do not see how rules apply, except in terms of the treatment of prisoners. In World War Two, driving an ambulance on the battlefields of Europe, as civilians me and my mates, if captured, risked being shot as spies. We should be grateful that the Geneva Convention decreed that prisoners should not be shot.

This evening David and Judy Mason are coming to us for a last minute scratch supper. Except that Jenny's Fish Pie is, actually, a gourmet dish.

Saturday ◈ MARCH 22

We did not share much sensible discussion last night, although we did have a brief word about the disappointing political scene in the UK, and also about Obama, Clinton and McCain. I sensed that David would like the next US President to be the latter which suggests that he is a diehard Conservative. I am critical of my friends. I am also self-critical, and I say to myself you are an ordinary Joe, but what are you really like? Through my genes I have always been a bit of a Thespian. I often like to perform. I seek an audience, which means of course, that like all actors I want to be appreciated for what I am, and have a need to be liked, if not loved. Despite my passages of outgoing friendship I find that I am not liked or loved. I am perhaps tolerated, but for the most part I am written off as a chap of no particular interest. Bit unfair! After all, I am also a bit serious with a streak of the North country puritan in my veins. I am a questioning Quaker and critical of the apparent dumbness of political party leaders. Will humankind ever understand the crying need for tolerance, compromise and peace? And the need to settle differences not with guns but with words?

Sunday ❖ MARCH 23

To a packed church with shoals of children because the holiday people are in town. The children took up most of the one hour service. Minister Brian entertained them and gained their participation in examining the meaning of the Cross and the resurrection. There was much laughter but not much time for actual worship, unless you regard the entire service as Holy. I miss the stillness, the quiet of a Quaker Meeting for worship.

At 1.00 p.m, we went to Peter and Sue for lunch and found Euan Harvie-Watt seated in the conservatory and in fine form. We took Sue a bottle of white wine from Verona, an Easter egg and some of my roasted cashew nuts. We enjoyed an excellent red pepper and tomato soup, with roast lamb and well-cooked vegetables, followed by raspberry crumble, ice cream and cheeses. I excused myself at 4.00 p.m. as I wanted to watch TV. There was a recorded interview with Anthony Minghella, the Oscar winning film Director. (He died about a month ago. A great loss to cinema.)

Monday ❖ MARCH 24

Julian James rang this morning to let us know that Margot Anderson died at 7.00 a.m. There is grief, but also great thankfulness that Gavin and the family can finally come to terms with this frightful tragedy. In effect, hard as it may seem, we all thank God for this deliverance. This does not, alas, take away the dreadful void that her passing leaves, and I cannot imagine how Gavin and his family will manage. They have waited in dread and with little hope for five terrible weeks.

Father Magnifico has sent a message to say we should pick up, on line, a Reuters account called 'Bear Witness.' Five years of slaughter and mayhem in Iraq is shown via pictures and accounts from Reuters journalists and camera crews. It is a remarkable and terrible account of human suffering. Those who support the madness of war should be made to witness this document. The news today reports that 4,000 American service personnel have been killed in Iraq so far. I don't think anyone really knows how many Iraqi civilians have been killed, but the fact is the true number must be many hundreds of thousands of men, women and children. And to that figure there must be added the many thousands who survived but were terribly wounded. Reuters cameramen lost their lives in showing the carnage. Their courage should be saluted.

This afternoon I made a start on destroying files and paper in the conservatory. But I kept treasured books on urban planning by that genius Gordon Cullen with whom I spent so many hours. He was my hero. I still exchange Christmas Cards with his widow Jaqueline, a French noblewoman. She knew, and I knew, along with a few architects, how ground-breaking Gordon's work was. Did Nehru not ask him to re-plan Delhi.

Tuesday ◆ MARCH 25

I took 80 minutes to make Sweet Potato and Coconut Soup this morning. Too slow. One big onion thinly sliced and cooked in butter. Three big sweet potatoes chopped into small cubes then sweated in butter with cumin, cayenne and a little ginger, a pinch of sugar, and a twist or two of pepper. Add the onion to the potato and cook very gently in a pint of veg stock to blend them. Wait until nearly cool then whizz to produce a creamy consistency. Add contents of a tin of coconut milk, bring to a brief boil then cool the soup in the fridge – perhaps overnight. Ready? If you are a woman don your best sari or grass skirt and sing a nice song from Mali or Jamaica. If you are male. just your y-fronts and an apron, and do the Jump-up, 'Back to back and belly to belly in a Jumbie Jamboree!' Invite Barak Obama and serve (the soup) hot or cold in your best bowls.

After an early supper Jenny is off to a church meeting. I am reading Pip Martin's 'Experiment in Depth' which draws on the work of T.S. Eliot, Jung and Toynbee, the Historian.

Wednesday ◆ MARCH 26

We put Millie and Gemma in the car and off we went to Edinburgh to visit Goodwin's Antiques in Queensferry Street and choose the replacement signet ring. It was agreed that they would make one with a suitable blood stone. We then drove to Markinch where I bought wine at Sandy Stewart's Wine Gallery. Sandy is a former distinguished Cambridge academic in the field of Social Sciences. We thus paused and, leaning on a box of a dozen excellent wines which he had recommended, a learned discourse ensued. He conducted argumentation I could barely follow. Thence over to St. Andrews for a Thai lunch at L'Orient. Then Jenny went to Boots to get a face. Back home a message on the Ansafone told us that Sandra had died. She had suffered two severe strokes. That cloud of sadness still hovers over us. I sat down and wrote letters, to Gavin and family, and one to Sandra's husband Tom.

Thursday ◆ MARCH 27

I am dipping into Pip Martin's book 'Experiment in Depth', which includes chapters on psychological types, autonomous complexes, archetypal images, the individuation process, and the deep unconscious. It seemed almost child's play compared with Sandy's Social Sciences Wine Gallery seminar! Research today informed me that "Social Sciences are a group of academic disciplines that study human aspects of the world. They differ from the arts and humanities in that the social sciences tend to engage the use of the scientific method in the study of humanities, including quantative and qualitative methods." (Thank you Wikipedia)

Social sciences are 'soft sciences,' as opposed to hard sciences such as natural sciences which focus on objective aspects of nature. Apparently, the distinction between the hard and the soft is blurred. I wonder if this blurring brings academics into conflict, one with another?

Well, it is certainly blurring my brain! Examples of boundary blurring include disciplines like the social studies of medicine, socio-biology, neuropsychology, bio economics and the history and sociology of science.

Help! Get me out of here! I'm not going back to school. I'm with Mark Twain who said "never let school interfere with your education."

Jenny's world has taken her to the Golf Club to rehearse for a fashion show. Because she is tall and willowy she is to model golfing outfits and then have a light supper at the club. Probably lettuce. That is all models eat (apart from an occasional massive bif-steak).

Friday ◈ MARCH 28

Who needs TV, Radio or newsprint. Here in the village simply go to The Fruit Basket and you'll get the news. Today, in search of bananas, chillies and a melon I met the one and only Valerie Fraser who shrieked "He won! Three firsts and two seconds!" (Horses). "He will be richer than ever! "I yelled back, referring to Peter Russell.

"Champagne! "she cried. "And he met McCain's misus. y'know, next President of the US. Can't raise his arms y'know, war wounds, prisoner y'know!"

"I'm for Obama," I said.

"No NO!" she shrieked. "They'll cut his throat! Kill him! SNIP! He's, y'know. "

"Black," I said. "A Nigger?"

"You can't say that," cautioned Carol, joining in.

"Or Golliwog! shrieked Valerie.

Carol said "We were in the South, Memphis Tennessee, and everyone, but everyone down there says Nigger!"

"I look forward," I suggested, "to meeting the first black Captain of The Golf House Club."

The Fruit Basket erupted in a chorus of "No! NEVER!"

I left in haste with the melon, bananas and chillies in a plastic bag. Amazing really, to find such prejudice in a fruiterers shop in Scotland AD 2008. The denizens of this place by the sea are lovely people, but clearly headed for Hell.

Saturday ◆ MARCH 29

At 6.00 p.m. we drove through torrential rain to Edinburgh to attend Dick Harden's 70th birthday party in the Royal Scots Club. It was a cheery occasion and among some 50 guests we met Edinburgh friends we had not seen for years. Alison Long was there as buxom and bouncy as ever, and it was a delight to meet Cousin Sue and Jim from Eyemouth and, of course, Sarah and Ginny, Dick's two daughters, both wild, and beautiful. We consumed a good deal of champagne, then sat to a super supper.

Home and to bed at around 1.30 a.m. (having put clocks and watches an hour forward). Come on Summer!

Sunday ◆ MARCH 30

Took Rosina to Meeting. Then TV. Body and mind resting. Still no Summer.

Monday ◆ MARCH 31

It WAS Summer in the conservatory – 90F by mid-day. But it was also Margot Anderson's funeral. A very large number of friends of the family attended the service in the village and raised their voices in The King of Love my Shepherd is, Be still my soul the Lord is on thy side, and Abide with me.

Gavin's daughter Margaret read ' On the Loss of a Loved One, and Gavin's son Guy made an excellent Tribute.

Father Salvo (Douglas Foulis) came over from Edinburgh to have lunch before the service and it was a joy to have him with us. After the service we all went as usual to the Golf House Club for wine, whisky, tea or coffee and sandwiches. Among those I met were Father Compressus (Oliver Balfour), Brigit, wife of Andrew Thomson (The Courier), Richard Simpson (MSP), Valerie Fraser, Alan Reid, Keith MacDonald, Donald MacDonald, Colin Ross, James Hardy from the West, Sue and Alan Mackie and a host of others, too many to name. There were probably 300 in the Club. I had a word with Gavin and Margaret, and Gavin said he would come to the Monks' Chapter on Monday where he is Father Aquila, the Fiscal. I was very moved to think that he would make the effort to attend. At the end of this day I felt utterly drained and so terribly sad for Gavin.

Tuesday ❖ APRIL 1

THE MAN FROM MARS.

I rang Bell Lawrie to ask whether they should sell half my holding in Rio Tinto to BHP Billiston (mining). There is talk of the two joining up to become one. A decision has to be made this week if I am to have the advantage of the £5,400 Capital Gains Tax exempt allowance. I told them to go ahead and sell. One can never be sure of the rights and wrongs in a time of financial turbulence. I gave them an analogy. Flying home a year or two ago the aircraft encountered turbulence and the Captain said: "The turbulence is severe and there is a danger of structural damage to the aircraft. I am taking us down to avoid trouble." So we descended a few thousand feet and came to no harm. I am expecting Bell Lawrie to do likewise, but even at a lower altitude there are no certainties. After all, shares or no shares, and Clear Air Turbulence or no, Life tends to find you out and it is risky, whether you are on a Motorway, in a plane or in a restaurant, or even in bed with your wife or lover! Computers too can be risky. Jenny is currently on the phone to someone in India whom, she hopes, can sort out an anti virus problem. She has been chatting for nearly an hour with the chap who says he lives in South India. He is called Sivaraj.

On Friday my Godchild Jo is to marry Jose Gonzalez at Smith Cove Beach, Grand Cayman, Cayman Islands. So we are sending an e-mail instead of flying out there. 'To Jo and Jose! We are sorry not to be with you in the sunny Cayman Islands. but send you congratulations. Be happy!'

Wednesday ❖ APRIL 2

The funeral of Sandra McCabe was attended by a great number of folk, most of whom we did not know. They probably came from Aberdeen where Sandra was born. She was 72 and until the terrible brain tumours were discovered she was a bright, outgoing and cheerful bundle of joy whom we all loved.

Thursday ◆ APRIL 3

This was the day we were visited by an alien in human form. The Man from The Milky Way. He came in response to a cry from Jenny for someone to mend her computer. He can peel away any faults on any computer as easily as peeling an onion. He clearly has several very sophisticated computers for a brain. He explained that humanoid medics had rumbled him, declared him to be Manic to the hundredth degree and had him sectioned. He obviously escaped, being far too clever for mere consultants. After an hour's conversation I was convinced that he was some kind of Angel with a brain we could not understand. After all, he said he charged only £35 for a call-out to humanoids no matter how long the visit took, anything from an hour to a week. As he swept his way through a million stops and starters on Jenny's machine he confessed his failings. He can build and/or repair any computer known to Man, but he cannot read a book. "I can read a sentence but when I get to the end of it I have to go back to the first words because I cannot remember them!" His passage from one Heavenly orbit to another enabled him to check out the computer which took the astronauts to the Moon. He said: "It was the smallest and SIMPLEST computer invented. With a larger and more complex computer there is more that could go wrong. Computers on aircraft are similar, the simpler the better." He has of course adopted a Scottish name, and he flies around mending computers everywhere. He says he lives in a house shaped like a boat. I don't believe that. His base is somewhere among the myriads of stars that you gaze upon in wonder on a clear, frosty night.

Friday ◆ APRIL 4

The daily news is not, or should not be an entertainment. Today we are reminded that it was 40 years ago that The Rev. Martin Luther King was shot. We killed the man who famously said "I have a dream." His dream was truly Christian, and bore fruit. Today we are also told that Tony Blair, a committed Roman Catholic of more than 20 years, is so worried by the planet's globalisation that he desires all our separate religions to become as one. Why? Because he says the world's power base is irrevocably moving from the West to the East. I think he is right. However, one is bound to ask that, if he is a true Christian how was it that he led Britain to invade, with the Bush administration, Iraq? The result was the killing of thousands upon thousands of civilians as well as service personnel. I am tempted to question whether the dangerous and destructive archetypal forces in his unconscious self have taken over. When this occurs beware of trouble.

I'll put my money on aliens. Early today the Angel from the Milky Way returned, with Jenny's computer completely cured. After a quick lesson on the required changes he has made, he left with his cheque for £35. "Any further problems, just press the right key" he said. "You can get me on your computer where I appear as a little green man." I was right! He IS an alien and knows precisely what is going on in Jupiter and Mars as well as our study here at home

Saturday ◆ APRIL 5

We drove to Crail pottery to buy Fraser McQuarrie his wedding present, and selected a beautiful salad bowl with servers and four little bowls to match. Down in the tiny harbour we then visited Mrs Riley's hut and purchased a freshly boiled crab for lunch tomorrow. (£2.80).

Sunday ◆ APRIL 6

Planned to go to Meeting but sudden snow rendered the journey ill-advised according to Jenny who went to church in the village. I followed down to the village to check the weather and at the last moment decided to stay back and attend the church service instead. Jenny's surprise was a delight to see. The church was crowded but I managed to find a seat beside Michael and Dorothy Dickson. There was a double Christening. two of the 15 grandchildren of the Irvings. Minister Brian was in fine form, reminding us that possessing lots of money did not necessarily lead to happiness.

Monday ◆ APRIL 7

The April Chapter of the Monks of St. Giles in Edinburgh was a crowded affair. Father Prior had returned from three weeks in New Zealand and I am sure all Fathers were impressed by the attendance of Fiscal Aquila, Gavin Anderson, so recently bereaved. He turned up as he promised he would, and dealt with business with the charm and efficiency that marks him out as a VSP (Very Special Person). I was called to say my lines and delivered 'Bangers and Mash.' Inevitably I was fined. I had to leave the Chapter half way through, but remained long enough to hear Father Nebulous (in great form) and a new Monk called Father Orpheous who said he would perform at the piano, a 'hymn' by George Gershwin! It turned out to be (of course) his Monk-ish verses sung to 'I Got Rhythm.' And yes, he had! My toes were tapping.

Tuesday ◆ APRIL 8

The Little Green Man from Outer Space, who has adopted the name of William Rowland, arrived with a Canon printer to replace the one we have had for some years and which ceased to function with my computer. He then spent half an hour setting up the replacement and when I asked him how much it cost he said £40! It was clearly a gift, as his call out fee was £35 of that £40. The equivalent machine from Canon would have cost more than £60. So now it is all systems go, as Jenny's computer is mended, and I have a printer with which to continue my journal.

This evening we are bidden to Peter and Mary Wang's holiday house next to The Ship Inn. Supper. I will take them white wine and roasted nuts.

Wednesday ◈ APRIL9

Peter and Mary were in fine form last night, offering glasses of white wine and, later, a very good island Malt. We ate rainbow trout which had been caught in a small loch near Tarbrax. Mary, curled up into a cuddlesome ball on the sofa, said "It came from our retired Postman, he is a very good fisherman!". Peter was as expansive as ever and told us about a fellow former Fettesian whom he met recently on Heriot Row, Edinburgh. They had been at school together but had not seen each other for years. Peter said "Y'know, there he was getting out of a slightly battered saloon car. He was wearing an equally well worn Barbour and you would never have guessed that he owned two whisky companies" (names withheld by editor). Peter said he was probably worth £300 million.

Thursday ◈ APRIL10

Today we have to go to St. Andrews to collect one or two items, now repaired, including my watch, while Jenny has to go to her oculist for eye tests.

Friday ◈ April 11

Three of our chairs require re-upholstering. After some discussion we agreed on a pattern we liked for one chair. Then, Jenny went off to play a medal while I coped with the dogs. Gemma barked incessantly. I tried to read, then gave up, and fell to wondering what on earth I was doing, or not doing, with my life. I started thinking about the vast universe and the folly or the beauty of it all. From time to time I contemplate those pillars of gas many trillions of miles high in outer space that the great telescopes show us spitting out matter that will make more stars. And then, my mind shifts to attempting to grasp the fact that (we are told) more than one universe exists.

The asylum is getting to me. I think I'll just watch The Masters in Sunny Augusta, Georgia. How many have made the cut?

Saturday ◆ April 12

Jenny had disappeared to a committee meeting in the Golf House Club, so I did the shopping and will do the cooking tonight. It will be a Thai Green Curry. Simple. Health-giving. As I prepared the ingredients, probably because of the rain, I invented a Proverb, as follows : 'Be like water – find your own level.' (Actually, I did. The curry, so easy to make, turned out to be ghastly!). Before lunch we went up to Cadgers Way to see Clare and her new-born baby. Mike Dickson was seated by the great picture window, his lap top on a table before him, and instead of the ugly boot on his foot with the fractured tendon he was wearing a pair of very smart black brogues. A sign that, hopefully, the tendon is at last healing. Seven weeks old Isla was sleeping soundly in her mother's arms, Husband Ralph emerged from work he had to do, and Colin, Caroline's intended was ready to cradle the baby as a good 'uncle' should, while Dorothy served the champagne. A celebration cake was cut. It had been made in the shape of a snowy ski-run, with the family figures all going down hill fast!

Sunday ◆ APRIL 13

Jenny went off to her morning Service and I drove over to St. Andrews Meeting. After 25 of us had settled in stillness and silence I got to my feet to offer a few words about Quaker Meetings for Worship to help visitors understand what we are about. People often ask "But what are Quakers? What do you do?"

I could have attempted an explanation in my own words, but felt it better to quote from a writer better qualified than me, so I spoke as follows:

"When it is successful, which is not always the Meeting is a method by which the deep centre is experienced and the experience is transmitted. How this comes about is a matter of surmise rather than knowledge. Partly, no doubt, it is due to the concerted seeking in silence. Since there is little to distract attention, the libido is free for inward exploration, for the discovery of The Kingdom. Partly it is attributable to the fact that in such Meetings there may be at least one or two present who in their own lives have gone over to the deep centre. They can help to 'take the Meeting down.' Partly (also) it may derive from the fellowship-in-depth of a 'gathered Meeting.' This sense of togetherness is a characteristic feature. In a Meeting that has 'centered down' there is simultaneously the feeling of the most complete unity and most complete individuality."

That, I find, is an excellent exposition and was clearly written either by a Member of the Religious Society of Friends, or by someone who had studied their ways. Put another way, the Meeting is simply a quiet hour in which those attending strive to empty their minds and hearts the better to be guided, to hear the still small voice which Quakers would characterise as the word of The Lord. We strive to obey the advice given in the 17th century by George Fox "To walk cheerfully over the face of the Earth answering that which is of God in everyone." I certainly find worship easier when there is a gathered silence than when the congregation in a church is so busy not only with readings from the Scriptures, but with an anthem, five hymns, a sermon and an address to the children. Even so, if I cannot get to the Quaker Meeting I sometimes accompany Jenny to The Church of Scotland Sunday Service.

Monday ◆ APRIL 14

Last night, in the late sunshine of Augusta, Immellman from South Africa did the business. As his competitors weakened and fell away he held on to triumph and to accept his Green Jacket in The Butler Cabin. The dream he had cherished for years came true, and surely no one could fail to be moved as he fell into the arms of his wife and family and held aloft his child for the world's cameras.

While I am not ambitious, I too have my dreams. I would willingly swop Emanuel Kant (and all that logic) for a roller-coaster run with Carl Jung. I sense 'dream therapy' has its good, if not vital, uses in promoting maturity and spiritual growth. To write down, or draw/paint a dream and then attempt to learn its meaning can be helpful. Jung would counsel that it is best to collect a string of dreams over a lengthy period before attempting to divine their meaning. A successful result would be to arrive at a better understanding of self of the whole man. I did not record the dream I had last night but I can remember it. In a landscape where a river ran a smartly dressed businessman was walking with a case which, I understood, contained a new battery – the kind that provides power for your car. I had asked a friend (Colin Ross) to procure such a battery for me, and I am sure that he tried so to do. But the businessman said unfortunately he did not have the correct type of battery for me. I paused beside the river. I was disappointed. I thought "Oh devil take it! I'll go for a swim instead." The river bank was steep but I managed to get down into the water and happily swam along with warm sunshine overhead. After a while I arrived at a point where the river ended at the foot of a building. There was nothing for it but to get out, so I hauled myself up to a window and, to my surprise, there was Jenny and another girl, very smiley and with long, blonde hair.

"Can I come in?" I enquired. Jenny and the girl smiled and said "Of course you can!" So I pulled myself up and climbed through the window. While I am not going to seek the meaning of the dream I suspect the battery I wanted represented my spiritual energy, or lack of it, and the waterway represented 'the River of Life.' I had swum to its end and, by entering the window I had found my grave as Jenny and her 'friend' (an Angel?) looked on.

Tuesday ◆ APRIL 15

To St. Andrews again this morning. Jenny had to select new frames for her specs, and we had to have a look at Farmore Interiors for alternative materials for those chairs. We ate lunch at L'Orient. I have asked the chef to let me have the recipe for his excellent Green Chicken Curry, and will collect it on Saturday when we attend the St. Andrews wedding of Fraser McQuarrie and his bride.

Wednesday ◆ APRIL 16

At 9.15 a.m. Jenny left to play the annual Ladies versus the Senior Men competition and will lunch at the Club afterwards. I was houseboy, shopping for fish, washing dishes, preparing a simple lunch of soup and cheese. And having a think. Here, beside the sea, we are barely a part of Planet 2008. We are on The Playground of Advanced Years where friends teach golf to their young grandchildren and all seems well with the world. Drugs, rape and murder with knife or gun is reported via the news, but we are not in an urban area and we do not feel to be part of that world. (We are unbelievably fortunate.) Much of the world community appears to have lost any interest in what many would regard as sense and spirituality. And, it is the Banks, and monumental corporations, not Governments, that rule. Money is indeed the God for most people today. Pessimistic? Well, can you be otherwise as warnings tell us that as the world's population soars there already is a severe shortage of food for vast numbers of people. Prices of basics such as wheat and rice are shooting sky high. Today, millions strive to survive on what amounts to less than two handfuls of rice a day. If the power brokers like IMF and the World Bank would get wise it need not be so. They would of course require the co-operation and fair-mindedness of political leaders in Africa, China, India and elsewhere, but alas, what hope of that? Our black cousins will not even condemn dictators like Mugabe. And it is thus that the suicidal charade plays on in a haze of mayhem, violence and misery. The Pope, Gordon Brown and Bush are meeting at this very minute. But, to what end? The Pope simply seems to be apologising for the thousands of his priests who, for many years, have sexually abused young people.

Thursday ◆ APRIL 17

Fifty years ago a wise man was writing on the human situation when the cold war was still 'hot.' In the present age, he wrote that the world was divided against itself. (Quote) "Both sides are piling up the means of mutual annihilation. The free peoples pin their faith upon the possibility of finding some basis of peaceful co-existence, an agreement to live and let live. But this is to ignore the very nature of our troubles. Mankind is divided not only politically but morally."

I agree, and that is how it still is, today. And the writer continues, to say "Manifestly what is needed is true wholeness. We have to rediscover the creative contact, find again the living source." (By which, as a Christian as well as a Jungian, he means God). And he adds "As Nietzsche put it: God is dead. But Nietzsche was mistaken, it is not God who is dead. It is we who are only half alive. But the effect is essentially the same. We are cut off."

Friday ◆ APRIL 18

Last night Val and Anne came for supper. I had warned them that the menu would be Thai curry, and they responded with enthusiasm. Val gave us an account of his holiday which included an extended tour of the North and South islands of New Zealand as well as Malaysia. When we had demolished the chicken curry and moved to pudding I wanted to talk about politics but could draw no wisdom from either of them. Except that Anne said "They will kill Obama, he'll be shot." This worried me. Here is someone else convinced that Obama will not become the President of the USA even if he successfully negotiates the final hurdle

A letter arrived from Jane and Jim Carstairs who live in South Street. It contained a cutting from yesterday's Daily Telegraph with a short column headed 'Drummers could be natural brain boxes.' Well, of course. I totally agree!

Saturday ◆ APRIL 19

Before attending St. Salvator's Chapel in St. Andrews for the wedding of Fraser and Emily we called in at L'Orient for another taste of Thai Green Chicken Curry. After lunch we walked round to the chapel but could not immediately enter as the Kate Kennedy Parade was just starting out from the Salvator's quadrangle. A unique and colourful procession, it dates from the 1840's, but a similar parade was held as far back as 1432. Organised by the University's Kate Kennedy Club the parade features the many historical characters of the town. The students dress in their ancient colourful robes; some ride horseback; there were coaches too. It was bitterly cold for the immense crowd of spectators and we chose our time to dash across the road and in to the warmth of the chapel. The standard wedding service was enhanced by the singing of a student choir in the gallery and they did a good job ending with the Flower Duet from Lakme by Delibes. The hymns were Praise my soul the King of Heaven, Amazing Grace, and an accelerating, invigorating Give me Joy in my heart. Emily looked very pretty and happy and was attended by five Maids, three of whom were Doctors like her and two were young Lawyers.

We all then drove over to that monstrous building which used to be called the St. Andrews Bay Hotel and is now The Fairmont. We ate our way through a long menu. There were speeches. They should have used microphones, I could hear little of what was said. As a drummer in a Band I get to a lot of weddings and it is usual for the speeches to be too lengthy. At one wedding in Edinburgh some time ago they were so long there was no time left for the usual dancing (we were paid for doing nothing!)

Today I received a second cutting from the Daily Telegraph suggesting that Drummers are 'brainboxes.' This one came from Raquel and Nicky. So I sent them another Proverb I have invented, as follows: 'It is a wise man who knows where his trousers are.'

Sunday ◆ APRIL 20

Letters. Then cooking a veg mousaka. I reflected on how we are often busier in retirement than when we worked the five-day week. As a journalist in Fleet Street I simply drove into town, parked on the Embankment and walked through Temple to the office. No cooking, just lunch in the refec. Or canteen. Or Pub. When, after night duty, at 6.a.m. I drove home by way of the flower market in Covent Garden, I stopped in a Pub for toast and brandy. Later, when working in the Advertising business, I drove from my flat in Hampstead to the office in Berkeley Square, and ate lunch in a nearby Pub, or a restaurant in Charles Street or Bond Street. Later still, in The City (Moorgate), we had our own restaurant and chef on the 17th floor and entertained our clients there. So, in a lazy way, life was simpler. My secretary even parked my car for me!

Monday ◆ APRIL 21

Today, HOORAY! We cleared the conservatory, moving cupboards, table and chairs into the garage and started on the unenviable task of sorting out files and papers. Old photographs, letters and poems. And a few memories.

Tuesday ◆ APRIL 22

Today the thoughts of millions turn to the State of Pennsylvania. To the people of Pittsburgh, the industrialists and the people of the Allegheny uplands and the good, the bad and the ugly sandwiched between Ohio and New York State. They vote either for Hillary Clinton or Barack Obama in the big Primary. I prophesy a narrow win for Hillary. But if she makes it big there with a crunching win it could spell trouble for Obama. So, fingers crossed. We need Obama.

I did not dream of politics last night. Instead I found myself walking in an open landscape with Dennis Pilgrim who was an assistant Features Editor in Fleet Street. It rained and we sought shelter in a pub whose name I cannot recall. "My shout," I said. "What will you have?" He answered, to my surprise "champagne!" I said I had not sufficient money on my person for that. "No matter," he replied. "I am having a party tonight and I have plenty of the stuff."

As the day progresses I will sort yet more files. I feel we are moving rapidly to some sort of end, or beginning. The global financial crisis reveals the suicidal lust and greed for power and money by the big corporations and political power brokers, not least our Banks which are having to be baled out by The Treasury to the tune of £50 billion. Meantime, the emerging nations, the have-nots, will want what the West still has and, following our example, will hasten the downward spiral. By attempting to get food for 80 million or more starving people, by creating more massive industrialisation (China, India, Africa et al) the wrong route will be followed and disaster will result. The question is can the young people of the world do better and put the Doomsday scenario to bed. Or will they also suffer starvation, violence and greed.

Wednesday ◈ **APRIL 23**

Ouch! I had hoped Hillary Clinton would win no better than by 5 or 6 points. This morning it is clear that she has won by at least 10 and kept her bid for leadership very much in the frame. Commentators are still insisting the outcome of the contest is too close to call, even though Obama is regarded as remaining in the lead.

Yesterday the German visitors to the house next door looked in for a glass of wine. Barbara with her three year old daughter Hannah, and Ulrika (grandmama). Barbara speaks good English so we could communicate, but it was playtime for Hannah so conversation was limited. Barbara's husband had returned to Germany. "His business," she said. "He sells houses."

Today we are bidden to The Toft for supper with Magnus and Dossie with their daughter Connie who is four, and with Mary another grandmama. We will take smoked salmon, prawns and a bottle of wine.

Thursday ◈ **APRIL 24**

We had a pleasant evening yesterday with Magnus, Dossie, Con and Mary. Dossie is pregnant (due September) and looking as beautiful as ever. Magnus, in full throttle, was an admirable host. He is the boss of BMW for Edinburgh, and I asked him how the credit squeeze was affecting business, by which I meant Sales. His answer was positive. "Not at all, we are expanding and have just purchased four acres to the West of the city."

The cure for over-indulgence of course is golf. So this morning I went out for a few holes, but after six the rain rudely interrupted play. It would be encouraging to have some good news for a change. But, Alas! It is reported that in England and Wales two and a half million children are missing school because of the teachers strike. Thousands of schools are closed. A strike is also threatened in Scotland In this case it is the workers at the Grangemouth oil refinery who may walk out unless they too obtain the pay rise they are demanding. Just in case, like many others who have to depend on their cars, we went to the filling station in Colinsburgh. Yesterday the pumps were empty, but today a tanker re-fuelled the station.

Friday ◆ **APRIL 25**

Eleven holes on the course today, and I am beginning to swing a five wood. Jenny played in the Ladies' Holm Cup and won it, bringing her handicap down by three points! The next door Germans called in to say goodbye. They return to Cologne tomorrow.

Saturday ◆ **APRIL 26**

The Grangemouth refinery will close down tomorrow for two days, and, worse still, the pipe line (oil and gas) from the North Sea fields is to be closed. Petrol will thus be less available and the Government is appealing to us all not to stock pile the stuff.

To lunch, with the chattering classes, at The Lea Rig, holiday home of David and Elizabeth Simpson. Excellent food and wine, and a great chat with Richard and Christine Simpson, Michael Barratt (in wheel chair) Robert Burns, Colin Ross, Geoffrey and Vivi Millar.

Sunday ◆ **APRIL 27**

As primitive people in years long gone would say, 'The Gods are laughing!' Yes, indeed. The Gods are the Chess Masters and we are the Pawns, the Kings and Queens, and we are being mercilessly moved around the black and white squares. Mate and Checkmate are no longer in our hands, it is the Gods who call the moves. Already their Angels are uttering 'Mate', and I fear that Checkmate will follow very soon for, in all that we can divine, The Western World is in a mess. Today, The Sunday Times will publish The Rich List and it will be seen that the number of billionaires in Britain has risen by 15 per cent in the last 12 months. The gap between the very, very rich and the very, very poor has become a massive gulf. Meantime, the Western Governments continue to spend billions on war, while China and India, striving to catch up, spend billions on new factories, power stations, and cars, and thus help further to poison the planet. The Gods will not call halt and say (en effet) 'Okay people, if that is what you desire go ahead. We have given you free will and blessed you with a desire for Freedom. Furthermore, we have advised you how best to acquire The Good Life. If you are not listening, we cannot help you. Goodnight. And Goodbye.'(It is no joke.)

Pip Martin wrote "When freedom is threatened we spring to its defence. But, when freedom is secured we are at a loss to what to do with it. As a consequence, we win the wars but lose the peace. If we are ever to win the peace we have to know what freedom is for. Jung, Eliot and Toynbee sought new vision in the depths. They are, as it were, the spear points of a possible creative minority, dedicated to a new birth of freedom. At present though (Ed 1956) they are spear points only. The question is whether and how, on the basis of their discoveries, the peoples of the world can find the means of creative renewal. The author later continues:" Mythos meant originally the words spoken in a ritual, the means of approach to God. Jung's constructive technique, Eliot's mythical method, Toynbee's withdrawal-and-return are so many modern means of approach to the creative process working in and through man.'

What was written by Pip Martin half a century ago seems to me to be wholly relevant today. Quite apart from in-depth psychology, maybe, and only maybe, some new form of science could take us out of our un-Holy mess. Meantime, down on our knees. And pray.

Monday ◈ **APRIL 28**

Five Star Shepherd's Pie is not as simple as cookbooks suggest. The one I am making, supervised by Masterchef Jenny contains minced beef and a harlequinade of chopped or sliced vegetables, including green pepper, onion, mixed herbs, parsley, leek, carrots

PLUS flour, Bisto, chicken stock, red wine, salt, pepper and nutmeg and a sprinkle of sugar. The potato topping is mashed with butter and seasoned. The whole thing will be served with broccoli and some baked beans.

Wednesday ◆ APRIL 29

Brilliantly sunny and almost warm. In the conservatory with two windows open the temperature soared in the middle of the day to 40 C. We had to drive to St. Andrews, Jenny to her dentist. I collected cinnamon and coriander from Rogers, that excellent little shop in South Street which, in common with quite a number of other shops in town, is to close due to a steep rise in rates.

Once I tried to do a surgical job on the word Faith. Now I wanted to do the same on the word Trust. But someone beat me to it and came with up this analogy: Think of Trust as a beautiful vase of the thinnest and most delicate porcelain. Should you break that vase in a rash or clumsy moment you can always find an opportunity to attempt to put the pieces together again. BUT the vase will never be quite the same as it was. Several pieces were too badly damaged to be of use, so the vase can never again shine with the beauty it originally possessed. Such is the word Trust. I suppose Trust is what nations most require when attempting to negotiate one with another.

Wednesday ◆ APRIL 30

In retirement we usually have time to stand and stare. W.H. Davies, the supertramp poet who died in 1940, reminded us in his verse called 'Leisure.' (Quote): 'What is this life, if full of care, we have no time to stand and stare?' (etc). But, as well as staring at outward phenomena, we can also stare inwards to learn more about ourselves. Then we can try to ascertain which is the strong side of ourselves and which is the weaker side. Such discoveries can be misleading. For myself I suspect the stronger side is the inward side i.e: the realm of dreams and creativity. And I guess we have all played the game of What would you like to have done if you had your days over again? I think I would choose to be a successful novelist, or an actor, or an architect. Or maybe even a Clown.

Thursday ❖ MAY 1

A HUMAN DISASTER

May Day brings memories, and for a moment I was in Oxford again by the bridge as the choir welcomed the sun and as I found the punt, tied a bottle of Gordons to the stern and poled away. Round a bend in the river a trad Band was swinging. Some of the best jazz I had ever heard. Today, here by the sea the sun appeared so I celebrated by swinging in a different mode and played nine holes. Jenny was in the Town Hall on Church affairs so later I went down the Pub for a swift half. I then called at the pharmacy and on an impulse bought perfume for her.

In England and Wales local elections are in full swing. In Fife today all is peace. I found myself thinking of Paris in May, of the passionate philosophy and political café table 'discute.' There is/was a saying which in translation means 'under the paving stones, the beach, Yes, of course. But, what shows on the surface does not reflect what is going on below, treacherous quicksand, or a stony way, or footsteps in the cooling sweetness of a shallow tide.

Then we had music. 'It can lift your spirits and soothe your soul.' Thus read the programme for the Scottish Chamber Orchestra's 2007/08 Season in St. Andrews' Younger Hall. So, after an early supper, we drove away to hear this marvellous orchestra salute Beethoven, Mozart and Schumann. Conductor Louis Langree.

Leonore No 2. Boom! Boom! went the timps fortissimo before strings and woodwind slid their way into mystery and sadness and fantastic colour, every colour under the sun. Mozart's Sinfonia Concertante ushered us into the withdrawing room for tea with best china and suitable wallpaper and, of course, the lifting of a pretty petticoat unobserved as the chattering continued out through the French windows. However, most guests remained to listen spellbound to the loving – and the agonising – exchanges between viola and violin. Okay Wolfgang Amadeus, we are always game for more, especially when Louis is conducting. My God! He embraced his musicians, he attacked them, he blessed them, he wafted them to Lotus lands, he crouched, he leapt, he boldly had them in his hands. Then, Herr Schumann. Symphony No 4. After the solemn and regal opening it was, simply, pure nectar.

Friday ◆ MAY 2

Jenny had to spend almost 7 hours in the clubhouse and on the links. I had to mind the dogs. Gemma managed to knock the large glass bowl which contained the last of the fish pie to he floor. It shattered of course. A difficult day was rescued by our visit to David and Judy for dinner. Mike and Dorothy Dickson had also been invited. Judy made lovely food, and David produced a truly professorial port. We largely avoided politics except to note the Labour Party's terrible results in the local elections in England and Wales, and the defeat of Ken Livingston for Mayor of London by the young old Etonian and comic Boris Johnson.

Saturday ◆ MAY 3

The Spring Meeting today, so the links was crawling. I had to repair to the wee nine hole course. Some rugby on TV. Bath hammered Saracens. In the evening Jenny supervised my Green Thai Curry with prawns. The result was awful.

The Labour Party is moaning about its defeat in the local elections. David Cameron is over the moon. Now, all politicians, irrespective of Party, are swearing that they will "listen to the people." But, "the people" is such a pot pourri of opinions, of sense and utter nonsense that I cannot see what good the listening could do. Perhaps an ear to The New Testament would be better.

Sunday ◆ MAY 4

Quaker Meeting today was suitably quiet, but Robin spoke well about Quaker work in the Sudan among the refugees. Then, there's poor Mr. Brown. How long is it going to take today's Labour political 'king-makers' to realise that to be a successful leader of a Party in Britain today you have to have a bright and shining persona, the humour of Bob Hope, the charm of Parkinson, and the youth and looks of Prince William.

Monday ◆ MAY 5

Today Jenny and I will drive to Edinburgh and then on to Muirfield by Gullane where she will deliver me at the club gates to play in Pipelli, the mad golf round that takes place each year and is played exclusively by The Monks of St. Giles. Some 20 of us are expected.

Tuesday ◆ MAY 6

Yesterday I was at Muirfield by 12 noon. It was business as usual: practice rounds of gin and tonic, or Pimms or beer as Monks assembled. Lunch followed, the excellent food tempting appetites. When we were ready for action Fr. Licarus produced a buggy and invited me to join him. "We'll just play nine holes," he said. "Your partner is Fr. Aquila (Gavin Anderson) and I have Fr Auditorius (Tom Usher)." Of course! Fr. Licarus is a cunning old owl. He tees up his ball on the fairways and can hit it about 20 paces. Tom plays off 9 and can fly the ball straight as an arrow and out of sight. It was not hard to guess which couple would win. I did little to assist Gavin. I experienced a severe pain in my right foot. It was so bad I had to remove my golf shoe and play one–booted! After tea with toast and Gentleman's relish, Fathers re-assembled at the Golf Inn for Shepherd's Pie. The voluntaries (verses) kept us awake – but only just – until 10 p.m. when Fr. Penurius kindly drove me back to town to rendezvous with Jenny who had taken supper with Kathleen and Chico Ramos at No 2 Kilmaurs Terrace. Home by 1.00 a.m. today with Millie and Gemma who, Jenny said, behaved admirably for fully ten hours with her.

This morning Jenny is playing in The Moroccan Salver. In Burma it is a little different. A cyclone has destroyed much of the inhabited parts of the Irrawaddy delta. Numbers of dead are not yet known but the figure will probably reach 30,000, with an additional thousands 'missing.' The military junta which rules this private nation should accept aid from the rest of the world. Much of the country's rice crop is in ruins. Appeals for help are world-wide. This is a catastrophe. The news from Zimbabwe offers little cheer with Mugabe still intimidating the rural population. He lost the recent election but refuses to stand down.

Wednesday ◆ MAY 7

Good news. Barak Obama has had a decisive win in the North Carolina Primary, and ran Hilary Clinton very close in Indiana. She should now pull out of the contest, but I fear she will not.

This morning I reminded Jenny that we should have another crack at clearing up in the house. It is over-filled with stuff we simply do not use, or need. There is much we could take to a charity shop.

It is another sunny 'Summer' day. I wish Finesse would arrive to start work on the conservatory, and have sent them a hurry-up reminder. I have also had to remind More-Than (Insurance) to send the cheque to me for the signet ring.

Late news: The Burmese government is not allowing aid agencies to get food and water to survivors. If permission is not granted there will be a second disaster larger than the first. How can we bear to think of this.

Thursday ◆ MAY 8

"The spirit of man is the candle of The Lord." Who wrote those words? I am so uneducated I have no idea, but what a remarkable sentence it is. It is near to being a Quakerly concept, because Quakers say there is that which is of God in everyone. It is the Light within. And we are encouraged to heed that light.

I have just asked Jenny if, as an Elder of the Kirk, she might know where the spirit of man quote came from. She had no idea, but dipped into her computer and came up with the author. It

80

turned out to be a Dr. Jack Hyles (who died in February 2001). He was the Pastor of the First Baptist Church of Hammond, Indiana which has a membership of 100,000.

Friday ❧ MAY 9

The Cardinal Roman Archbishop of Westminster has called for a dialogue between Christians of Faith, and non-believers. I am not sure of what use that might be, but he is making sensible noises. If we want a better, a safer, a fairer world we have to accept that there are things in Heaven and Earth which (as Hamlet told Horatio)" are not dreamed of in our philosophy." The Archbishop is right, of course. No one can prove logically that God or Christ exist. Logic may have legs and make rationalisations, but it will take you only so far. The rest of the journey has to depend on Faith and Trust. If we cannot practice those two concepts the world will never know peace.

Jenny has gone off to the golf course and the club for the day. I have just returned from a half hour session with Suzy Delaney. Today, she accompanied the therapy with a song because she knows I enjoy music – and she has a good voice!

Saturday ❧ MAY 10

"It's a coffee morning in the Church Hall for Christian Aid," said Jenny. "Are you coming?" I said Okay. The hall was packed with white haired ladies drinking coffee at the many tables, and there were other tables offering flowers, books and home made cakes. Also a raffle. Later, I took Jenny to lunch at the Ship Inn. Then, At 5.00 p.m. with the kit in the car, plus the dogs, we drove over to Tayfield, the home of William Berry, for the celebration of his two sons, both of whom had married within months of each other. The marque in the garden of this 18th century estate was the size of two tennis courts. It was divided by a curtain separating the dining area from the dance floor. We set up our gear then joined the guests (at least 200) to drink champagne and scoff quails eggs in celery salt, mini Yorkshire puds with horseradish, nobs of chicken in a Thai dip and other delicacies.

The dinner menu showed a starter of Wilde Thyme of sea trout – hot-smoked sea trout on a spring pea puree, tartare with quails egg and caviar. Mosaic terrine with blood orange. The Main was Loin of spring lamb with confit lamb shoulder and creamed wild garlic, morels, broad beans and pancetta with a pimento and caper jus. Dessert followed – Apple tatin with calvados and cinnamon ice cream, then coffee and organic tea. Good nosh which would keep us going for the reels and jigs. Dashing White Sergeant, Eightsome Reel, Waltz, Hamilton House, Duke of Perth and the always popular Reel of the 51st Highland Division. We were joined on the podium by three extra fiddles, including Donald Macdonald, chairman of the Scottish Chamber Orchestra. The guests danced in seemly fashion. They seemed happy. A standing ovation. Jenny was an excellent roady and also a guest – but no one asked her to make up a set. Perhaps just as well. She had to walk and water the dogs in the garden where the bougainvillaea flamed darkly, lit by golden chains of lights in the trees and shrubs. We left at 12.30 a.m. and were back home for bed at 1.45 a.m.

Sunday ◆ MAY 11

The news from Burma is even more alarming than before. The military junta are still not allowing aids agencies to distribute the vital supplies of clean water, food, medicines and other necessities and there is talk now of thousands likely to die of disease. Mountains of relief aid are piling up on the borders of the country. What a terrible contrast it all is against the celebrations last night by the silvery Tay which does not float with dead corpses. Last night was simply a family celebration. There is no gain in guilt but we feel awful.

China and India could do much to rescue millions, but they hold back in a kind of silent duel, each nation vying to become the prime power broker in this part of the world. Bloody politics.

Monday ◆ MAY 12

Home news features the government's refusal to find extra money for caring agencies struggling to deal with the mounting numbers of the aged and disabled in our communities. It is a serious problem and will get worse each year. It could be solved if the government would siphon off a billion or so from the slush fund that finances new nuclear submarines and fighter aircraft. After all, the government's pot of gold profits enormously from the sales of arms world-wide. Politics and morality are not easy bedfellows.

As Jenny swung her way round the links I went down to South Street with a letter of thanks to Jim Finlay for giving us some home-grown asparagus.

More bad news. Not far from embattled Burma an earthquake (7.8 on the Richter scale) has hit a remote county in China. So far five schools have been demolished and the death toll already is given as 8,000. It will undoubtedly be much higher when relief teams get through into what is a mountainous area with roads and bridges destroyed.

Tuesday ◆ MAY 13

It is now clear that China faces a monstrous human disaster with 12,000 killed, and thousands more under the rubble, with towns and villages completely raised. Vast numbers are injured. Many more will die. Meanwhile, in Burma the rescue from the cyclone is slow with the government insisting that only they can distribute aid. It is different in China. The response has been fast and professional with thousands of trained troops working with aid agencies from around the world. It would seem that, as humankind continues to destroy planet Earth (eg: demolition of the rain forests) nature has declared it will lend a hand and speed the process with earthquake and flood. Perhaps we will need another Noah's Ark.

I have sorted several hundred postcards showing drawings that I made eight or more years ago and never sold. Perhaps I should attempt to market them, they are no use left stacked in boxes. My only creative achievement today was to write a letter to David Todd as he continues on his way to becoming a Minister of the Church of Scotland. He will do well.

Wednesday ◆ MAY 14

This morning four very large men arrived, men both wide and tall and with strength enough to lift a 15 cwt. truck! They ate breakfast in their van, then started to demolish the frame of the conservatory. By 1.00 p.m. the old framework had been removed, and one of the giants said the new frame would arrive tomorrow.

Meantime, in the real world the work of rescue continues in China. In Burma the Monsoon rains are pouring down, hampering the aid teams there. And in the Home Counties there are stories of sightings of visiting saucers from outer space, with little green men. The government has released visuals of 'something.' TV reports from China show that in the province affected, with a population of 85 million, the humanitarian disaster gets worse by the hour. Aid cannot reach the hill towns and villages despite the efforts of 100,000 extra troops being drafted in. The roads have been destroyed and militiamen are having to advance one by one on foot. Thousands of victims will never be reached, the death toll will soar and the putrified corpses, in the warm, wet weather will inevitably give rise to disease and many more deaths. We have no conception of what it must really be like as the militia strive to rescue the dead.

Thursday ◆ MAY 15

Today Prince Charles has made a plea for the retention of the world's rain forests. He has clearly been excellently briefed by his scientific advisors.

Friday ◆ MAY 16

Ten hours of brilliant sunshine, and no wind until 6.00p.m. when it turned to the north east and we were chilly. Garden grass is green and sappy and shooting up, and again that light, golden as

Bollinger, streams across the links where Jenny was playing in the Kathleen Glover with Anne Riddle and Mary Warrack. They did not win. But then, neither did Sally Watson (plus two), or her sister Rebecca (minus one).

I played ten holes on the wee course. Later Jenny told me she had purchased two books that will make good reading: The Mitfords – the letters between the sisters which throw light on that other world between the two world wars. The other book is Andrew Greig's latest novel called' Romanno Bridge'. He is a wonderfully talented and poetic story teller. And this one is a thriller.

Saturday ◈ MAY 17

What a pleasure it was to hear General Cordingly on the radio this morning. Not because he led The Desert Rats in World War Two, but because he is one of the few people these days who speaks the Queen's English. So many people simply mumble and mutter. We should all pronounce our wonderful language proudly and properly. What the General had to say also made sense. He advised that, instead of condemning the Burmese junta out of hand for their refusal to allow aid from the Free world into their country, we should seek sensible dialogue with the Generals who rule. Above all, we should remember that they have a different culture to us. The fact is we have gone some way down that path and with no success. As for China, the Government there is doing an admirable job under terrible circumstances. Apart from the dead and dying some 5 million people are now without homes.

Sunday ◈ MAY 18

Half an hour to Meeting, driving under a cloudless sky through the lanes and hedgerows green and fresh and tender. It is the best time of the year before boughs become heavily clad, mature and darkly green.

In the square, twin-windowed Meeting Room some 30 Friends sit together to share the deep silence which is not easy for me. In the stillness my imagination plagues me as visions like vivid dreams persist. I have attended Quaker Meetings for Worship since my teens and my daft brain should know better. I picked up the book of Advices and Queries, opened it at a random page and read:' We are called to live in the virtue of that life and power that takes away the occasion of all wars. Do you faithfully maintain our testimony that war and the preparation for war are inconsistent with the spirit of Christ? Search out whatever in your own way of life may contain the seeds of war. Stand firm in our testimony, even when others commit or prepare to commit acts of violence.' Okay, that's pretty tough when you look into the asylum today. But whoever said that Christian faith was an easy option.

Monday ◆ MAY 19

Both China and Burma have declared three days of mourning and three minute silences in remembrance of the tens of thousands of victims of the earthquake and the cyclone.

Here at home our silence was broken by the arrival of the joiners with the framework of the new conservatory. I was on the golf course for almost three hours and did not notice the work in progress until mid-day. Then, alas! I saw that the hardwood frames had been painted white. We had agreed with the supplier that the hardwood mahogany would simply be varnished. We despatched an e-mail (to Finesse) and late in the day received a call from the boss (Thain). He replied promptly with an apology. "It was my fault," he said. "Very sorry. I will have the paint removed. They can do it on site." As we are paying some £16,000 we are determined to see the job done as stated in our agreement.

Tuesday ◆ MAY 20

To the surgery and Dr. Clare Francis. There she is, as immaculate as ever, willowy, smiling, attentive, welcoming, the best advertisement for the NHS one could possibly hope for. My appointment lasted only three minutes but I would like to have lingered longer.

The Pinehurst event for tomorrow has been cancelled. We are relieved as there are busy days ahead with Thursday and Friday in Edinburgh where the Band will be playing at Fettes College for the annual fund-raising dinner and dance for Scottish Adoption.

At around 2.00p.m. Neil Thain (Finesse) turned up, chisel in hand, and apologised again for the painting error and said he would get a man down tomorrow to start removing the paint.

Wednesday ◈ MAY 21

We are an asylum, and the madness continues now in Moscow where many thousands of English football supporters have poured into Red Square in anticipation of tonight's European Cup Final between Man. United and Chelsea. Russian police are taking no chances should trouble erupt. There will be no fewer than 2,000 police within the stadium and many thousands patrolling the streets outside. And the money? Millions for both teams, win or lose.

Five million people are homeless in China. How many in Burma? And in Darfur some 2.2 million, mainly women and children, are homeless and the women are still being raped by the militia.

Thursday ◈ MAY 22

Jenny took the dogs to the kennels early this morning, then with the car loaded with all my kit and her golf gear we drove over to Murrayfield where she will play in the Ladies Invitational with Sylvia. I drove round to The Gallery of Modern Art for a look at an exhibition which mainly featured an artist called Bevan whom I had never heard of but who became the chairman of H.S. Benson, the Ad. agency in London during the time I was with JWT in Berkeley Square.

On the other side of the city I took Chico and Kathy some lovely bread and a bottle of Sauvignon from Marlborough, NZ. Then back to Murrayfield to pick up Jenny and take a swift half of Belhaven Best with Sylvia and Les Girls. Then it was off to Kinnear Road to Rachel and Nicky in their splendid new home.

We took them their supper of asparagus and Chicken Dijon, and cheeses.

In the Crewe by-election Labour suffered a massive defeat. More mayhem for Mr. Brown. Some of his Cabinet want him to stand down. But he won't.

Friday ◆ MAY 23

Errands in the city. We also collected my signet from Goodwins. For lunch we visited Chez Pierre in Eyre Place. Busy. Noisy. Jenny chose bangers and mash and I ordered mussels. After a three-hour rest in Kinnear Road we changed and ate a splendid Band supper prepared by Rachel for Peter and Sheila, Iain and Sally, David Todd, Ian King, Jenny and I and Nicky. Thence to Fettes College spacious dining room to play the familiar gig. Halfway through the evening an attractive young woman in a black dress dancing an Eightsome blew me a kiss, so I waved back Later, while I was seeking water for the Band, she came up to me and said accusingly "A year ago you promised to come and see us, but you didn't!"

It was Karen Archibald with whom I had once organised a charity Ball. Now I recognised her and apologised. "Promise me! We must get together again!" I promised, whereupon she handed me a slip of paper bearing her telephone number.

At 1.00 a.m. after Auld Lang Syne, Jenny appeared to help pack the kit and drove me back home. Bed by 3.A.M.

Saturday ◆ MAY 24

Jenny to her committee meeting at ten. I bought scallops. At 6.00 p.m. we went to Euan H-W's for drinks and to see his daughter Jenny, sister of Catriona who was one of our brides-maids at St. Cuthberts, Edinburgh, and who now lives in San Francisco. Across a crowded room we enjoyed the young and old familiars.

Sunday ◆ MAY 25

Jenny to church. I wrote a note to Karen Archibald and reminded myself that a promise means nothing until it is delivered.

Luncheon with Alan and Susan Mackie. We took them chocolates and some of my roasted cashew nuts to accompany Alan's Chablis and/or Pimms. Susan had made a fantastic and delicate assortment of canape. We ate cold salmon (Alan had caught the fish) with salads and vegetables, followed by fruit salad and ice cream from a bowl fashioned from ice which Susan had made. Then chocolates. Cheeses, coffee. I sat at table with Louise MacDonald and a delightful woman I had never met before. I believe she was a psychologist. Afterwards we all strolled out into the gardens. Parties hereabouts are always noisy and companionable, and Alan and Susan produce the best.

Monday ◆ MAY 26

To David and Sheila Peebles for supper. David was most generous with libations of wine which loosened my tongue and encouraged me to discuss dreams and the deep unconscious. I caught his interest when I said that such is the timeless country of the collective unconscious that some of our dreams are no different from those that were dreamed by prophets and seers in Biblical days.

Tuesday ◆ MAY 27

Supersonic flight is no longer available. Concorde's terrible disaster when it burst into flames at take-off ended that incredible advance in aviation history. But I am sure supersonics will return in due time. After all, humankind has just succeeded in landing an un-manned space probe on the planet Mars which is now sending pictures back to planet Earth. A remarkable achievement which was in my mind as we drove over to Fortune's Field to take a trip on the grounded Concorde at Scotland's National Museum of Flight. We met Chico and Kathy at the hanger and were handed our boarding passes. I was astonished to see the size of the aircraft, an unreal, vast white bird. It was the miracle of the Sixties, and is now old-fashioned. And it was, as we knew, a slim craft with a narrow aisle between twin seats on either hand. In fact it was so narrow that only very, very slim stewardesses could serve the caviar, lobster and champagne. As we climbed into the cabin with our handsets we were able to listen to a commentary describing the craft's features. We were not allowed on to the flight deck but could view it through a glass screen. There was a work station for the flight engineer. One of his tasks was to move the fuel around the aircraft to maintain correct balance in flight.

Wednesday ◆ MAY 28

Jenny went to Pilates. Later, we discussed arrangements for the Curtis Cup in St. Andrews. Jenny wants to go to the opening ceremony tomorrow.

Thursday ◆ MAY 29

Conservatory almost complete. The joiners left after lunch. Jenny had church work and then at 5.00 p.m. she left to watch the opening ceremony of The Curtis Cup. A Pipe Band is promised, and a choir from Madras School.

Friday ◆ MAY 30

Jenny, Jean and Sheila left early for the Curtis Cup. For me, reading. I started on the letters of the six Mitford girls. Jenny reappeared soon after 5.00 p.m. The good news was that 'our girl' Sally Watson and her partners won both their matches.

Saturday ◆ MAY 31

This morning I spotted a family of what I think were starlings. They were in pairs and the darker of the two was feeding its partner, beak to beak. They pecked and fed as a family.

That giant man-made 'bird', Concorde, certainly raised my eyebrows last Tuesday, especially when I saw one of its jet engines displayed separately among other exhibits. I was simply amazed at the human skill and ingenuity that the engineer designers must have possessed in the 1960's.

On the Old Course Sally Watson has now won three out of her four matches. We drove to the farthest point on the course, one foot almost in the River Eden, parked and walked, intending to get to the stand by the Loop which gives a view of holes 10,11 and 12. But it was too far. So we turned tail and drove to the Eden Clubhouse car park and walked over to where we could observe the 14th green and the 15th tee. The three matches came through. Putting was abysmally slow, but on the 15th tee I was able to stand within two yards of the girls swinging. Americans and Brit alike were very smart and 'focussed.' I was amazed at the speed of their swings and the distance they drove. The Sally/Krystle pairing was a total success.

Sunday ◈ JUNE 1

"MICHAEL, I LOVE YOU!"

Jenny is off to the Church today. I will remain at home. This Sabbath began with a surprise. I was in the kitchen and glancing from the window I saw a sudden movement in the next door garden. Three horses leapt over the fence to Miss Munzie's top lawn.

Jenny returned from the golf at 5.00 p.m. with the news that the Americans, as expected, walked it, winning by 13 points to 7.

Monday ◈ JUNE 2

To Edinburgh this morning for the Monks' June Chapter. I have been put on the Fiscal's rosta so have to have a contribution to read if I am to avoid a fine. My muse is not hot but I will offer a short piece entitled 'Cold Comfort.' It is my 2008 version of the 13th century Anon verse and refers to the annual pilgrimage which Father Prior takes.

Sumer is NOT icumen in
Lhude shout Boo-Hoo!
The Haar is cumen in instead
An' blockin' oot the view.
Oh, do not blow thou gale force wynd
It chills us to the core
An' leaves our sunny days behind
There'll no be any more.
The climate change moves on apace
Globe warming is the curse,
Wi' Summer snow upon your face
It canna get much worse.
As for lovers during May
There was no ding-a-ding,
Wi' frozen arms an' legs an' hearts
They couldna' love the Spring.
Be WARNED, dear Monks, in cold July
As Pilgrims you'll be chilly,
An' langan tae gang ony place
You'd be a Silly Billy.
So, if the Prior makes us roam
Outdoors in freezin' air
I trust he'll foot the Bill and pay
For our thermal underwear.

I have been writing rubbish like that on the first Monday of every month (except two) every year since I was made a Monk in 1986. (Some 200 verses) As subjects for our rhymes and songs Politics, Sex, and Religion are not allowed, but occasionally I have done Sex and been fined several pence.

Tuesday ◆ JUNE 3

To the Professor, for Sicilian wine. Thence to St. Andrews for Jenny to see the Consultant dermatologist in the wee hospital. She has a facial spot which her GP said should be attended to. The Consultant gave it the inevitable squirt from his can of 'rocket fuel' and said he would scrape the spot away in a week or so. It is the same treatment that I had when the dermatologist at Ninewells scraped my scalp.

Wednesday ◈ JUNE 4

I note that Rome has just been visited by Mugabe who lost the election for the Presidency of Zimbabwe but refuses to stand down and has again lectured the West for causing the abysmal mess his people face, They have no money and many are starving, or have fled the country. At the same time it has been declared today that Barack Obama has now won the battle against Hilary Clinton and will lead the Democrats in the November play-off against McCain. Although Clinton has been defeated she also refuses to stand down. So what's going on? The votes go against you, you lose the contest, but continue as if you had won it. Of course. It could only happen in the asylum.

The frame for the conservatory will be completed today. We will be .£16,320 poorer, and have still to bring in a painter and decorator before we can re-furnish

Thursday ◈ JUNE 5

Dogs to the kennels, and at 12 noon we drove North to Sutherland, via Perth. Brief halt at Bruar to buy asparagus then on to Inverness, over the bridges to just short of Golspie where we turned off to Rogart and up a single track to Dalreavoch Lodge near Strath Brora. We were welcomed by Colin and Elaine Ross and shown to our bedroom. The Lodge is about 100 years old, very comfortable with two sitting rooms, dining room and a spacious, modern kitchen. Also the luxury of a cook and a housekeeper. The two Gavins and Anne were also there, but were leaving the following morning.

Friday ◈ JUNE 6

With Colin at the wheel we drove away on a scenic tour down deserted Strath Brora and the lonely, beautiful loch to the coast and to Dunrobin Castle near Golspie. We clambered up and down stairs, stared at portraits and glassy-eyed stags heads. It is a Victorian pile. Very ugly. But from the windows on high the gardens looked superb lit by sun and sea light. We then toured down the coast to Dornoch and dallied in that wonderful cathedral, originally built by the Bishop of Caithness in 1222. We stared at 28 stained glass windows and found two fat ladies seated at the reception table, beaming and happy in their religion. Then it was back to the Lodge. We sat outside and drank wine. The peace and the space stretched out Time. Time became endless. Even the weather held its breath. Warm air. And in the trees not a leaf stirred.

Saturday ◆ JUNE 7

Another Lodge breakfast with eggs easy over. I surprised Colin and Elaine with a short reading from 'Experiment in Depth', that very special book based on a study of the work of Carl Jung, T.S. Eliot and the historian Toynbee. It was first published in 1955 but is as relevant today as it was in the time of the Cold War. I have promised to lend it to Elaine.

We then said farewell and drove back to Fife, pausing only for a lunchtime bowl of soup outside and under a warm sun at Bruar.

The day ended with drinks at the home of Keith and Carolyn who were celebrating five years of marriage. Then on to the Ship Inn for fish and chips with Jen and Alan Corbett.

Sunday ◆ JUNE 8

Off to St. Andrews to collect Irene and take her to lunch. She had been driven up from Heysham in a taxi, a journey she makes every year. This is her seventh visit which is usually preceded by a card which reads "Michael I love you, I must come to see you." Until we renewed contact seven years ago she had been seeking me for years. She is very tall and today was wearing dark trousers and a flirty pink blouse. It transpires that her family lived on a large Baltic estate near Kolobrzeg where her mother never paid for anything except with "bars of gold." She is the great granddaughter of a Nobleman, the equivalent of a Duke. Her family was completely destroyed by the invading Russian army in the second World War. She lost everything, became a penniless refugee, refused to join the Hitler Youth and amazingly got away unharmed. Somehow she survived persecution and the Nazi death camps. Irene describes herself now as English, refusing to acknowledge anything and everything that is German. She bears herself with dignity, and appears still to have money. I noticed that each of her drop earrings today contained four beautiful diamonds. We took her to Rufflets Hotel for lunch after drinking red wine on the sunny terrace and discussing the spiritual life. She is a devout Roman Catholic.

Monday ◆ **JUNE 9**

Today TV showed us the beginning of the grass court tennis season at The Queen's Club. It also showed us the number of British service personnel so far killed in Afghanistan. Exactly 100. The public is beginning again to voice its concern about the value of the war in that troubled land which supplies about 90 per cent of the world's heroin. Heroin and terrorism, it is explained, are the reasons we are wasting money and service personnel in that mountainous, arid, dust-blown territory. People now doubt that much progress is being achieved. Even if The West succeeded in ending the drugs cartels there they would simply spring up elsewhere. It is much the same as prostitution and arms dealing, these activities (if under attack) would simply go 'underground.' Our money and soldiers would be better employed in helping to ease the water shortage and famine in war-torn third world countries.

Tuesday ◆ **JUNE 10**

Irene again. This time we took her for lunch at The Dolls House. She said "I eat only fish." Irene also advised us that "I drink now only red wine, it is good for me." We ordered accordingly. Today, she was not as cheerful as before. She insisted that we should go to visit her at home in Heysham where, in her library, she says, "I have a nice picture of you, Michael!"

She repeated that she possessed "Oh – so MUCH! Pictures and furniture and the pictures are by a famous artist who painted Adolf Hitler yerrrs!" She realises that her life is coming to a close and that she must put all her possessions somewhere. Her best friend appears to be a neighbour who is in the Fire service.

"Oh, he is so kind to me, and helpful. Oh. I have now yes a new gas boiler, it is so much work and everything I do, in the garden, oh-oh! So MUCH!" She complains, and sighs and has long silences which I attempt to fill. Her English is pretty limited. She likes to recall how we first met. She can remember everything, while I can recall very little except that I picked her up on the beach when I lived in Brighton and travelled daily to my job as a journalist in Fleet Street. She had come to England for a holiday as a young student. I had moved to Brighton and was single, having broken with my wife. I knew no one in the town so that when my News Editor directed that I should cover new shows in London while our regular arts critics were up at The Edinburgh Festival, I eagerly obeyed. I was provided with two tickets for various First Nights, but had no one to take with me. That was why, and how I met Irene — I needed someone to make use of my spare ticket. I asked if she would like to accompany me. She agreed. It seems that I took her to several theatres, also to The Ballet at Covent Garden where I had to write about Fonteyn and Beriosova and other Prima Ballerinas. After phoning my crits to catch the first edition we ate in restaurants in Soho, and The Ivy and in The Press Club. Irene remembers this and much more. She says "Yerrs! You introduce me to Lord Beaverbrook! I know everything we do, you were so kind to me, Michael, it was wonderful, yerrs! I remember ALL!"

She knows my birthdate, also what we ate and drank, my small flat in The Royal Crescent on the seafront, and how we played draughts and drank cider. "Always draughts, yerrs! You are allowing me to win!"

She was a most attractive young woman, and had become a teacher of painting in Hanover. After all that she had survived she had suddenly found freedom in England. It must have seemed like Heaven to her.

I still wonder if we were lovers, but she assured me more

than once that we did not sleep together. It was simply that "You were so kind to me Michael, yerrs ! I never forget it."

After searching for me, when at last, as instructed, we made contact, it was in the Bar of The Russell Hotel on The Scores, St Andrews. The place appeared to be deserted, but there, against the blaze of the far window, was the dark silhouette of a tall figure. A voice called "Michael!" "Irene? "I answered. And stepped forward into the Past.

Wednesday ◈ JUNE 11

Ah! The green (and slippery) grass at the Artois. Nadal, Rodick, Hewitt, Djorkovic, Mahut, Murray, Safin, Nalbandian. Jenny used to play at Queens. So did Alan (my brother). I had to be content with Northern tournaments, the Yorkshire Juniors and the North of England. And playing for Man. University. Alan and I once had to play a Davis Cup couple. Of course we lost. I was supposed to play at Junior Wimbledon but the war cancelled the event. Later, as a journalist I had some compensation. My newspaper regularly sent me to cover the championships. Free tickets, strawberries, iced coffee, and interviewing the stars.

Thursday ◈ JUNE 12

Son of The Manse, and key performer in the Band, David Todd was once the manager of an hotel in Nairn. Currently he organises the Edinburgh Festival opening Parade and now hopes to become a Minister of The Church of Scotland. So perhaps it was no surprise to find him standing at a Bar with other tall figures. We were encouraged to leave his hide-away and climb a nearby slope. It was tricky, but once up there we discovered an oval bucket probably made of canvas. It contained no water and we were worried because workmen on a nearby scaffolding needed water to remain strong enough to do their job. Happily a friend turned up and offered us a drink. There was no glass or mug so I simply had to cup my hands and try to drink the 'new' water from my fleshly container.

Not all dreams are reflections of the outward, conscious life.

Maybe they come from a deeper source. To understand what that dream meant I will probably have to wait a while. But if I had to interpret it here and now I would think the empty bucket represented the aridity of my everyday life. Then a friend (David?) arrived and encouraged me to drink, to take the real water of Life and find spiritual refreshment.

Friday ◆ JUNE 13

It seems to me that we are not helped by Ministers and other wise people who say "We are saved ! All will be well in the end! "For, when I look across the asylum, when I receive the news of what appears to be happening here and in other lands, I sense that, indeed, the time of the asylum has arrived. Of some things I am convinced. Acquiring a large mansion, or many mansions, a Bank balance of a million or two, rich food and wine and rich friends do not lead me to be 'whole.' I fear it may be more rewarding to attempt to acknowledge my weaknesses in addition to any strengths I possess. I may believe that there is that of God in everyone but, what then? Have I the will and the energy to act on that knowledge and understand what it demands of me in my daily life.

Saturday ◆ JUNE 14

Having re - read yesterday's entry in the journal I am alarmed. But I had better keep on trying to walk that high wire of Faith.

Sunday ◆ JUNE 15

When we were in Sutherland I promised to lend Elaine 'That Book.' And I will do so. But before I hand it in I thought I had better warn her, and so wrote her a note.

'Dear Elaine,

That Book

I do not want you to feel you have to read it. You may wish to read only part of it. (Initially, it scared me to death!) Its conclusion leads towards the striving for human 'wholeness.' Inevitably, therefore, for us in the Western world, it relates to the Christian Way. It concerns, in psychological terms the need to reconcile (to join) the unconscious, inner side of ourselves to the outward side, the 'ordinary' world in which most of us live.

You appreciate that to live only and entirely in the outward world (ie: the world of telegrams and anger) is less than useless, concerned as it so often is with greed, the lust for power, for domination (etc) which spring from egotism and the misuse of such freedom as we possess. The result leads to hypocrisy, lack of trust, and to wars which then create starvation, tyranny, slaughter and a kind of universal unhappiness and dissatisfaction as to who we are, why we are on a planet called Earth, and what we should do about it. The book is not an easy read. It is tough. Its scope is enormous as it signals the dangers as well as the benefits of seeking 'the deep centre' that collective, unconscious area of the human psyche which is so largely disregarded. The book is not dogmatic. It does not offer certainties, for there are none. But it does attempt to signpost a way if you wish along the rocky road to Faith. I liked the author's quotations, and especially the one heading Chapter X11 'Great truths do not take hold of the hearts of the masses. And now as all the world is in error, how shall I, though I know the true path, how shall I guide? If I know that I cannot succeed and yet try to force success, this world is but another source of error. Better then to desist and strive no more. But, if I do not strive, who will?

Chang-tse, Fourth Centuary B.C.

Monday ◈ JUNE 16

It really does seem as if the British government has taken leave of its senses. More troops are to be poured into Afghanistan to attempt to cope with the Taliban. PM Brown has just made the announcement. We see on the TV screen shots of British troops firing round after round at something they cannot hit or see.

Brave men of course. But, how many more will be brought home very dead in black bags? How many more interviews will there be on TV showing grieving mums and dads being asked stupid questions by journalists "a terrible loss. How do you feel now?" How, in all that is mad. are they expected to feel, having lost a son (or daughter) in the dust and terror of a foreign place. Meantime the politicians mouth soothing words "We will bring the boys home just as soon as we can." Lies. Rubbish. As for President Bush, he is reported as saying please kill Bin Laden before I retire, will you. (He clearly wants his war activities to appear justified before he retires).

For Britain, and America, and other warring countries, I suggest a better plan would be to pray to God for this folly to cease. Anyone should be forgiven for believing that, in the year of Grace 2008, the so called civilised world, is seriously in error. Of course it is. We live in an asylum.

A report on Iraq: 4 million refugees. *Report on Mugabe: he refuses to give up his presidency even if he again loses the election. *Report on marriage: two Church of England Ministers (both male) are married in a City of London Church, causing The Anglican Communion yet more grief.

Tuesday ◆ JUNE 17

This journal is becoming too grave, too heavy hearted. One reason must be that it is not simply the rattle of an ordinary man. It tries to look beyond the confines of one humanoid and ascertain what on earth is going on, day-by-day, in the asylum.

Wednesday ◆ JUNE 18

Yesterday and today we salute the magnificent horses and the colourful jockeys. The owners and trainers in morning suit and toppers. The thousands of spectators crowding the enormous new stand, with the other fillies, the women, parading their eccentric hats, and placing bets on the colour of the Queen's hat which changes day by day. Royal Ascot of course.

I once donned a topper and a morning suit for an outing with

Jenny and my in-laws, binoculars and champagne to hand. Even got a smile from Princess Margaret. Ascot is a seductive occasion, a vision of 'the upper classes' in the Royal enclosure. Five days of hugging, back slapping, joy and disappointment. And then, if you pause between races, that other world intrudes. The repeated reports from Afghanistan where the Army is being reinforced to help repel and destroy the Taliban, and where blameless young men (and women) are being killed. It is war and it is dirty, despite all the courage clearly shown. The action is reported daily under a banner headline which reads 'For Queen and Country'. 'Well, there goes the Queen with Prince Philip in their landau, pointing and waving to the country, and preparing a generous smile for the ten quid punters.

Last week, in a far country, five gallant young soldiers were slaughtered. Today, another four. One of them a woman at arms. Here, nine families that did not go to Ascot as their children, lauded and praised, went to their graves. A decent Irish Lieut. Col. was not smiling. "Inevitably," he said, "there will be casualties."

Thursday ❖ JUNE 19

Today, yesterday and tomorrow here in Britain, houses are being re-possessed as families cannot keep up the mortgage payments. House prices are falling drastically, but with the 'credit crunch' and fears of a serious recession there is not sufficient money on the move. The big Banks are wobbling. Meantime, them as is wearing toppers and sexy fashion at Ascot on Ladies Day well, they aint worried one little bit. "Pop another bottle darlin'! "

This evening Ian and Marcia will call by to take us for a dose of culture at Dundee Rep where the brilliant ensemble is performing 'Les Parents Terrible.' Lots of incest. I don't think we will like it.

Friday ❖ JUNE 20

Au contraire! Ann Louise Ross, Emily Winter, Kevin Lennon and John Buick were startlingly good, and the play, brilliantly directed and designed, upheld the Rep's universally acknowledged excellence. We laughed, rather than groaned. On returning home I sat down to write a note for Marcia and Ian, but found I couldn't. I switched on the TV before turning in and caught the news. Another report on the young servicemen, and the woman, who had been blown to bits in Afghanistan. How can we sleep when this madness continues. It is bravery and blood in a far land, with little achieved.

Saturday ◆ JUNE 21

The Summer solstice. The longest day of the year which means that Summer has, officially, begun. Grey skies. Chill winds. Downpours forecast! The news is so utterly gloomy I should try to practice laughing. The only people I can see laughing are the toppers at Ascot who own a horse that won. The rest of us can cry into our beer.

Tonight we go to The Hub (Edinburgh) to play a gig for Elizabeth Fairbairn and her friends. After setting up our gear we are to have supper by kind permission of David Todd in his splendid apartment on the High Street.

Sunday ◆ JUNE 22

For reasons too numerous to mention we would not be eager to have this year 2008 back again. It seems a typhoon has hit a ferry in the Philippines, possibly 229 drowned and thousands injured or missing. On land it has flooded towns and caused landslips.

Here, last night, after setting up all the gear David Todd gave us, and our wives, a delicious supper in his atelier. The long table was laid with fine China, Georgian silver, candelabra – and there were good wines. Then, to our amazement David said he had been rejected when interviewed for the Ministry. The Church of Scotland considered this man of all men unacceptable. We could not believe it. He is a son of the Manse, a Christian with academic degrees, he attends St. Giles where he sings in the choir. He possesses qualities of leadership and could charm monkeys from the loftiest canopy. He is a man loved, who loves, and is multi-talented. He will appeal against the George Street decision and we all sincerely hope that he succeeds.

Monday ◈ JUNE 23

Here, Wimbledon seems to be more popular than ever. At home just the usual chores. Plus thirteen holes of very bad golf. Venison and wild boar sausages tonight with mash. A few strawberries to follow.

Tuesday ◈ JUNE 24

Sigmund Freud would have had a field day. I was supposed to meet my brother Alan but could not find him. I knew also that I had an examination to do, a paper on mathematics which I could never understand. So I decided instead to visit a brothel. 'Madame' welcomed me and introduced a girl. "This is Maureen."

The girl smiled and said "Let's go for a ride, shall we?"

It was an open-topped Mercedes. Blood red. I took the wheel and off we drove to a cul-de-sac and a curved wall by the sea. We discussed cars and she said I would not want a different one "after this." We returned to the brothel and she gave a lecture on something and was warmly applauded by an unseen audience. After that we got down to the real business with groans and cries. I then had to collect my examination paper. It looked like a grocery list but mentioned several theatres. One line simply said 'Show.' It was underlined in red ink and was the subject for my essay. I said to myself 'Easy! It's a doddle!'

(Reference note): (a) In real/waking life I had written and produced a show called 'Just The Ticket.' I still have the text, the lyrics, the cast list, the sketches, the cost of costumes, the rehearsal rooms etc. We played for two weeks on The Edinburgh Festival Fringe. Once, slightly inebriated, I did visit Edinburgh's famous brothel which was across the road from where we lived. In a room with six beds there were six girls. They gave me a cup of tepid coffee and, pacing up and down, I lectured them on the wickedness of their ways!

I have always felt pretty ashamed about that. What a coward! I should have taken one of them to an upstairs room of pleasure then and there.

Wednesday ◆ JUNE 25

As author Andrew Greig might say 'Life keeps finding you.' So it does. Mainly to my discomfort. It seems that Life is as long as you want it to be but as short as it actually is. So – just accept messy. Birth, copulation and Death. But, what is actually'? It seems to me no good at all unless a Spiritual spark illuminates the mind. Today, I will try to hang on to Faith. As for the long and the short of it, T.S. Eliot had it beautifully when he wrote:

> 'For most of us, there is only the unattended
> Moment, the moment in and out of time,
> The distraction fit, lost in a shaft of sunlight,
> The wild thyme unseen, or the winter lightning
> Or the waterfall, or music heard so deeply
> That it is not heard at all, but you are the music
> While the music lasts.'

The idea of dodging life really is a myth. But Jenny and I did try when we fled London. We packed the two cars with all we possessed, popped into Covent Garden – a Royal Ballet matinee – and as the daffodils rained down at the final curtain we leapt into our cars and did not stop until we crossed the Border at Carter Bar. Escape? No. Life got us again as we turned into St. Bernard's Crescent where our days were to become just another hurdy-gurdy tune played in a different key.

Thursday ◆ JUNE 26

How hard it is to live each moment. To love each moment. Because, in your quieter time the thought slips into your mind that it is already too late to save the asylum. Perhaps us inmates, unknown to ourselves, are hell-bent on global suicide. The view of informed scientists – and even some lads down the Pub – is that unless communities, countries, nations actually succeed in establishing a low carbon economy the end is certain. So, on with the solar heating panels and up with world-wide windfarms. Otherwise, it is sure. We'll become a planetary cinder.

Tonight I am bidden to Edinburgh's New Club by The Rt. Hon. Lord Marnoch for a dinner to celebrate our good friend Dr. Peter Gordon, Muirfield Man and keyboard player in the Band. It is to be "a fairly small, male-only affair. Black tie."

Friday ◈ **JUNE 27**

A mild hangover this morning after the Dr Peter Gordon love–in on the top floor of The New Club last evening. Jenny delivered me, then drove away to have supper with Rachel as Nicky and I joined the G & T brigade and adjourned to the long room for dinner, port, and songs and stories. It was something like a Victorian 'Smoker.' with about 30 guests. I enjoyed the company of Ian Macmillan on my left and John Dudgeon to my right. The best entertainment came from Michael Farmer (excellent verse) and David Todd who ended the show with a virtuoso performance on his violin.

Saturday ◈ **JUNE 28**

I try not to steer my alleged mind, but rather let it steer me. Just wait. Quietly. And then walk the high wire. Which means Faith. That's the soul not the mind. Inevitably you keep falling off the high wire and when I do I find a soft landing. Cushions. And in a way, that's cheating. But, I do get up. I do try again.

This evening we will go to the Woodside home of Agnes where she has promised to feed Jenny and I, with Ronnie and Christine Sinclair and Alan and Jen Corbett.

Sunday ◈ **JUNE 29**

'He who hoots with the owl by night shall not soar with the eagles by day.' Quite a bit of hooting last night. Ronnie and Christine were not present but Peter Bucher and H-W took their places, with Eileen Waddell. Rich food, good wines, delightful house. But everyone talking at once is not beautiful. Shouting at the supper table often centres on IT, which is boring. But Agnes is a wonderful hostess, and her crème brulee fills me with delight!

This morning to Meeting, The little red book called Advices and Queries – the text of which was first written in 1700 A.D. – is always to hand and runs to 42 paragraphs. Today I liked the last one: "We do not own the world, and its riches are not ours to dispose of at will. Show a loving consideration for all creatures, and seek to maintain the beauty and variety of the world. Work to ensure that our increasing power over nature is used responsibly, with reverence for life. Rejoice in the splendour of God's continuing creation."

Yes. But there is also continuing destruction, witness Burma, China and other recent disasters with the loss of many thousands of lives. We are into tough times, and Faith (and that high wire walk) put Belief and Constancy to a severe test.

Monday ◆ JUNE 30

The Sunday Times 'Style' magazine is okay as an advertising vehicle for goodies that girlies like, shoes, frocks, arm candy, panties, perfumes and hair do's, plus an un-ashamed focus on celebs. The text tries to be modish. I read A.A. Gill's Table Talk feature. Most of it is rubbish, and yesterday he discovered the word Rumali which, he says, is the name given to the line of hair between a girl's navel and "her pubes." For his comments on food he had Jeremy Clarkson and Jemima Khan to his table in Soho and they shared "a plate of fresh sea urchin served on teaspoons resting on a bed of ice."

Clarkson said it was "exactly, exactly, not nearly but precisely like clitoris." The same issue of Style features an article on gynaecological techniques which are designed to make a woman's vagina after childbirth "tighter than a gnat's chuff," Evidently these "vaginal rejuvination procedures" are popular in America and France. You can also learn about having a proper bottom (whatever that is) and, to be fashionable you must cultivate the morning after look, ie: as if you had partied all night and were still wearing the same slaggy gear.

As for other topics in the asylum, Simon Jenkins writes " A growing body of critics argues that we must recognise failure in Afghanistan, and quit."

Tuesday ◈ JULY 1

WONDERFUL RARENESS AND JOY

It depends where you look in the asylum. Those who once loved us, and helped us, are taking their leave. Some 2,600 Aussie migrants are going home each month; 125,000 Polish migrants are now expected to quit our shores, and a further 179,000 foreign nationals are leaving. This suggests that we are en route to becoming a Third World country, a wet, grubby and overcrowded little island whose influence in the world, unhappily, is declining fast.

Wednesday ◈ JULY 2

I am trying to get Jenny to co-operate in clearing up our home which is so untidy. There is too much in this small cottage that we do not use or need and must go out to charity shops, to the refuse collectors, to a bonfire, ANYWHERE but here. I did get Jenny going this morning. She cleared some stuff off the mantelshelf in the sitting room. Among bits of paper was one on which was written (I cannot think why) 'The ivory-billed woodpecker has been re-discovered in dense woodlands to the north of Florida.'

Thursday ◈ JULY 3

Credit crunch. Banks are confused. Everyone is blaming "the global townturn." The housing and mortgage situation in England is in a mess. Homes repossessed, and on the health front the NHS, after 60 years continues to misuse the shoals of money we shovel into it. The Government answer? Build two more aircraft at a cost of billions of pounds. I cannot believe that aircraft carriers could do much to win, or end, the war in Afghanistan. Or help struggling families, and poverty. Or Third World starvation.

Here, the East Neuk Festival has begun. Tonight we will go to HolyTrinity in St Andrews to hear the SCO Strings and the

Orlando Consort. Bach's Brandenburgs 3 and 4 and some modern stuff.

Preparing for our Saturday night gig in the Festival, we dashed over to St. Andrews, early, shopped, bought a small BBQ in which to smoke the duck breasts we picked up at Millers. We then had to spend an hour putting the BBQ together, and get the heat going. The aim is a smoked duck terrine with which to feed the Band, plus a large green salad, chicken and smoked salmon. We have to drive to Kinkell Byre at 7.00 p.m. to set up, and then play reels until 1,00 a.m.

In the evening, after a Thai meal we walked round to Holy Trinity. On a stage between the massive stone arches and pillars were the brilliant musicians. I found Part's compositions puzzling, and sad, although the Consort's voices were very sweetly tuned. Then the strings and two flutes let fly with Bach's Brandenburg block busters. Total joy.

Friday ◆ JULY 4

And so they come from far and wide to find our secret places, these stony villages that cling to the shoreline, red roofs and slate and ancient walls, the empty shell of a fishing community not blasted by gales but lulled each summer festival by sweet sounds "that give delight and hurt not."

The winds today were different. The SCO Wind Octet in lofty Cellardyke Church. Beethoven and Schubert and Arvo Part's shadowy, haunted chords.

And there was more. At 10.00p.m we gathered by candlelight in St, Monans Kirk and found ourselves beckoned back to the 12th and 13th centuries with the chanting and ancient harmonies of the Orlando Consort. The sounds of Medieval Europe summoning in the mind the painted walls of the great cathedrals and monasteries, the kneeling Monks and the wide-eyed serfs adoring. The adorations were sung in Latin which, happily, were translated for us :

Blessed body of the Virgin Mary
To whose breast the King with the great name suckled

Under another garment concealing the power of your
. goodness
She dictated the creed for God and man.
O wonderful rareness and new joy
The integrity of a mother after childbirth.

(Perotin. Beata viscera).

And again there was more. The windows darkened and the
candle flames began to paint a flush of warmth on to the soaring
white arches of this most beautiful of churches. The four voices
of the Orlando Consort are known world wide and, as the programme tells, have won prestigious awards including one for
their work "on the extraordinary techniques of 12th century Aqui-
tanian polyphony." So, all hail to Matthew Venner (alto), Mark
Dobell (tenor), Angus Smith (tenor) and Donald Greig (baritone).
You astonished and enchanted us.

Saturday ◈ JULY 5

Jenny to her golf club committee while I meddled in the kitchen,
preparing that Band supper for tonight in Kinkell Byre. Prawns in
Marie Rose, smoked salmon, pork pies, special dressing for the
salad and so on. I left the dreaded terrine for better hands than
mine. But first, At 1.30 p.m., we went over to South Street to
attend the annual East Neuk Festival lunch with many other culture vultures in the summer home of Donald and Louise Mac-
Donald. A generous offering. A feast, with catering girls pouring
libations of wine. At least 50 of us spilled out into the garden and
to the sea wall for meeting and greeting and chattering and com-
paring musical preferences. Then home, replete and on the run at
5.40 p.m. to show Ian King the way to the Byre where Jenny set
out the Band supper in the Artists' Green Room' behind the stage.
The SCO's lighting and sound team wired our instruments in. I
was delighted to have four mikes on my kit. After all the checks
were complete The Auld Reekie Band settled for supper at a
round table, accompanied by the lady Caller and her husband. I
wondered if the dancers would need a caller. Then, until half past
midnight, we played for the guests, many of whom danced pretty

well, while the remainder took instruction from the Caller, mike in hand. We were back to bed by 1.30 a.m. but little sleep for me. After several hours of reels and jigs with my legs on high hat and base drum pumping the rhythm I was very sore.

Sunday ◆ JULY 6

Jenny early to church and coffee morning. I was grounded, but watched a bit of what turned out to be a Wimbledon saga Federer versus Nadal. The Final, was interrupted by spasms of rain. We then were transported by Colin and Elaine to Row 9 in the atrium of Fairmont, St. Andrews, where the SCO gave the Festival's farewell concert. Mendelssohn's music to 'A Midsummer Night's Dream', and Weber's miniatures from Oberon. We returned to have a light supper with Colin and Elaine only to find Federer and Nadal still hammering out the fifth and final set. Nadal triumphed.

Monday ◆ JULY 7

Yesterday's Sunday Times Magazine contained a reminder of Tony Blair, the Fettes College boy actor who chose politics as his stage until the final curtain after 10 years as PM. His new play, 'Peace broker in the Middle East' is still running but no one knows where to, or when and how the show will end. He regards himself as playing the leading role, and few actors have ever been as wealthy as he seems to be. He has very posh offices in Grosvenor Square (with a staff of 25), a £3.6 million house in Connaught Square, plus a £4 million country home in the Chiltern hills.

Tuesday ◆ JULY 8

News from the City of York where I was born. The Church of England Synod has been meeting there and the prelates find themselves confused. They have voted two to one in favour of women Bishops. There have been tears and some of the clergy will resign. There are fears that this gender issue will cause a rift that will divide the Church. The situation is not helped by economic stress, with those in the seats of political and financial power warning that the country is on the edge of a serious recession. The signs are manifest, with the building trade in trouble and having to lay off workers. There is an increase in knife crime on our streets and senseless murders. Currently, police are trying to find those who have recently committed a ghastly crime. In their rented flat two French students were bound and gagged, stabbed at least 200 times, then set on fire. There is a suggestion that this was done simply because their assailants wanted to steal their play-station games.

If the Churches do not remind us of our duties and responsibilities, and if the politicians and the police are unable to bring this mounting violence to an end, hope itself will become a fatality as people just look the other way, not because they are un-caring but because they feel powerless to help those who suffer.

Wednesday ◆ JULY 9

According to my first Diary (some years ago) on July 9th in Edinburgh Jenny and I appear to have been consorting with a bunch of Lawyers. It was the time when I had thought to start a small business making and selling quality quiche (!). QUOTE: It does not create a cool brow to bake five quiche before going out for supper. Our score: four Quiche Brigitte Bardot, and one ad hoc Jenny.

Then it was out and up the flagged path between blown roses to eat and drink with Gordon and Rachel (Fraser) and their friends. The decibels were deafening. Clearly a good party. The legal mafia were in full cry, and wolfing down massive portions of cold salmon, ham, turkey, salads of all kinds, strawberries and cream and gateau. We did likewise, then left at midnight to drive to the coast. Not every Lawyer at 50 gives such a generous and happy party (although I have heard that sometimes they remove all their clothes!)

I recall that Jenny and I were then both working five days a week so we had to make the quiche in the evenings. I styled myself as Mister G The Good Food Guy and we sold about £1,000 worth of our delicious product during one month at the coast.

Thursday ◆ JULY 10

Today, sorting out piles of books, I came across Prof. Simon Schama's 'Power of Art' which I read two years ago. His brilliant essays cover Caravaggio, Bernini, Rembrandt, David, Turner, Van Gogh, Picasso and Rothko. He quotes Picasso who said "Paintings are not done to decorate apartments; they are weapons of war." Viewing art today I think Picasso was right, and so is Prof. Schama. Here is a quote from the fly leaf of his book: "Great art has dreadful manners. The hushed reverence of the gallery can fool you into believing masterpieces are polite things, visions that soothe, charm and beguile, but actually they are thugs. Merciless and wily, the greatest paintings grab you in a headlock, rough up your composure and then proceed in short order to rearrange your sense of reality." It is a super book. The front cover simply shows a great splodge of blood.

Talking of blood, it is still being spilled in Afghanistan where 'friendly fire' has all but destroyed nine servicemen. And there will be blood letting in the football world. Man United's Ronaldo wants to transfer to Real Madrid. Presumably he wishes to move to earn more than his current wage of £120,000 per week.

Friday ◆ JULY 11

In two days the England Eleven playing against South Africa at Lords knocked up 590 runs or more with two centuries from Peterson and with Bell, being bowled and caught on 199. Bad luck. Neither did luck favour Colin Montgomery playing in the Scottish Open at Loch Lomond. He has failed to make the cut. Both cricket and golf are the best of our mid-year months.

Saturday ◆ JULY 12

Looking back at earlier comments in this journal it appears that Hope has again taken a holiday. We need, instead, to take a big breath, to stand up and start making the concept of peace and compassion come alive and make them a reality. I have to say that

Quakers (The Religious Society of Friends) DO try to hold on to sanity. This not to say that they are always right, or do not make mistakes, but at least they attempt to point the way to peace, to the ruling out of the crazy concept that the way to a peaceful world is by force of Arms. Not only do Quakers say this, they act on their belief, they refute violence and war. They put their money where their mouth is. Of course, Quakers can also be daft. We are often criticised for being dull. Example: My brother Alan in New Zealand says "Most Quakers do not read novels." If this is true, they are dismissing the wonderful gift called imagination. Odd. Because Quakers do like, and do make, music. These are dreadful generalisations. I make them because, even though most Quakers are Christians, and strive to follow the Biblical teachings of Jesus, so many people do not understand this, and look away, believing Friends to be un-worldly. History proves that to be utterly untrue.

Sunday ◆ **JULY 13**

At Meeting for Worship this morning Robin voiced a concern we may all share and which reflects the opposition within the Church of England to the appointment of women as Bishops. Although it is not our business, we would certainly welcome women Bishops. If George Fox were alive today he would have spoken out as well. A letter he wrote in 1676 contained the following: "Some there have been that would not have the women to speak without the men; and some of them say the women must not speak in the Church. And, if they must not speak what should they meet with them for? What a spirit is this that will neither suffer the women to speak amongst the men, nor meet among themselves to speak? For the power and Spirit of God gives liberty to all, for women are the heirs of life as well as the men, and heirs of Grace, and of the light of Christ Jesus as well as the men, and so stewards of the manifold grace of God." Any old how the C of E is getting it right. There WILL be women Bishops in due course and that is a good move. Their witness and guidance will enrich the Church.

Monday ◆ JULY 14

There has been wide media interest in Carla Bruni-Sarkozy, France's first lady. I have not read very much about her, but I like the idea of her. I would love to have met her, and at least she would have liked me because she likes Englishmen who have a strong femininity in them. So far, the Carla effect shines brightly. She is 40, a former model, she is Italian, she is wealthy, she is beautiful, she is durable, she is a song writer and musician, she has had many lovers and lives for love. Let me tell you, President Sarkozy, you are a lucky fellah! Perhaps she will inform your political style. As well as your bed.

Today, alas poor Gemma! Jenny has taken her to the vet. She has an inflamation on her left front paw, and is limping. She has been given an antibiotic. It is a breezy, sunny day so I clipped the hedge along the lane and at the rear of the garden.

Tuesday ◆ JULY 15

If you love your neighbour you can feel quite cheery. But what else helps to cheer up the asylum? For me, it is music. But not only yer actual Bach, Beethoven, Mendelssohn and Mozart, but the 'popular' stuff as well. Because that cheers us all up, young and old, rich and poor. Think of the great musicals: South Pacific, West Side Story, My Fair Lady, Oklahoma, Gigi, Cabaret, Gypsy, Evita, Cats, Phantom of The Opera, The Sound of Music, Funny Girl, Hello Dolly, Guys and Dolls, Fiddler on The Roof, Oliver, and many, more. Gypsy was one of my favourites, devised by Arthur Laurents, Jule Styne and Stephen Sondheim. I saw the show in New York with Ethel Merman as Rose, and the original cast. Today, alas we do not have musicals of that order.

Wednesday ◆ JULY 16

Uh-huh. Just the usual joy. Several hundred thousand public sector workers start a two day strike in England, Wales and N. Ireland. Pay, of course. And that aint all. For several days there have been complaints that vast numbers of childrens' exam papers are lying around unmarked. That is today's news. The news last night was that we took supper at Sangsters to Celebrate 37 years of marriage. We started with the famous twice-baked cheese souffle, Jenny then chose duck while I had an intermediate course (rissoto) followed by excellent halibut, and we both finished with a small crème brulee. With a bottle of House wine (£18) and service I had to stump up £103.80. In this village you have to pay for your pleasures. The next meal we give at home will be a Credit Crunch Lunch (bring your own teeth, and don't expect posh).

This afternoon we purchased a small table for the conservatory (which is now to be called The Bird Cage because of the wallpaper featuring birds among branches.) A Victorian delight.

Thursday ◆ JULY 17

The British Open at Royal Birkdale got under way this morning in atrocious weather, strong winds, rain and chill air. By the end of the day only three players were one under par. Ernie Els and Phil Michelson were 12 over and probably won't make the cut, and poor old Sandy Lyle found the going so tough he walked off after nine. Greg Norman was plus one. Age cannot wither him nor custom stale his infinite ability.

At tea time Jenny and I went down to The Toft, holiday home of The Wang Dynasty. Mary Wang (ne Maitland, whose family once lived at Lennoxlove) was over from Tarbrax minding Jane and Dossie's children, Magnus, Marcus, Connie, Inga and Lisabet. They were kept quiet by having their toe nails painted.

Friday ◆ JULY 18

Despite foul weather the golfing tyros battled on in the Open with the cut coming at eight over a par 70. The white shark led the field until little Mister J.K. Choi from Korea pipped him.

In the evening we went to Tigh-na-Mara to have supper with Geoffrey and Vivi Millar. We were eight to the table in the famous kitchen with delicious food, and good company. We roistered on until past midnight.

Saturday ◈ JULY 19

I guess that every village/hamlet has its own un-sung benefactors. I can immediately think of three: Hoover and Hoe, Gary our garden help, and Tom Macabe. But I am sure that there are more, including of course the Minister Brian. They enrich our lives. But, at the moment I am currently thinking of Space. the exploding universe and, well, who invented the supernova which is too vast to comprehend?

When people get a bit uppity and pretend to be superior, it is a good idea to remind them of where they live ie: on one of nine planets orbiting a sun which is just one of 200 billion stars in our Milky Way galaxy and which, in turn, is just one of an un-countable number of galaxies in the universe. So, how big do you feel now?

Tonight we are bidden to Marie Dougal's home to take supper with Eric Stevenson who is making his annual visit from Singapore. Marie's family, and mine, 'grew up' with the Stevenson family.

Sunday ◈ JULY 20

Marie gave us a very enjoyable supper party last night, and Eric was in fine form. With us was Hassie Young, from Bearsden who has a holiday home in the village. He is 92, a widower and former Banker and a most congenial companion. We were reminded by Eric that we are expected in a week's time to be at Edinburgh Academy with 100 or more of his friends for a dinner to celebrate his 85 birthday. This is one of his several venues, as he continues celebrating around the world.

This morning Jenny drove me to Meeting. It was felt unwise for me to drive there (as was usual practice) as I had had very little sleep. The dogs started barking at 2.00 a.m. so I was up and down coping with them.

As for the last day of the Open – Harrington did it. The player I most admired was Ian Poulter, the runner up.

Monday ❖ JULY 21

This morning Jenny announced that she would be "up at the Club" with more handicap work to prepare for a competition tomorrow. There is a bread you can buy called Tear and Share. In this household there is more tear than share as Jenny is so absent with golf work and with the Church keeping her occupied with yet more duties for longer or shorter periods, and often "all day." She has been away for hours in 115 out of 180 days. This includes golf matches, golf duties, Pilates, massage, dog training, photocopying, church and golf club committee meetings and so on. Someone said the other day " you are a golfing widower, Michael." Yes. The fact is Jenny is very self-sufficient, and this is a good thing because it will not matter very much when I am no longer in the asylum.

I was amused to see a headline in the Sunday Times yesterday: 'Lunatics take over Westminster asylum.' Yes, and not just at Westminster.

I am old fashioned, believing that a 'relationship' means togetherness, ie sharing quality time together, and having compatible interests. Today, we all want quality time but we seem to go our different ways to find it. Married couples, more often than not, both go out to work five days a week and can come together only at a week end.

Jenny is off again today to play golf and attend to the ladies endless handicap problems, and be present at a prize-giving tea. She does her duties very well, and for being so hard working and conscientious she is much loved.

Tuesday ❖ July 22

Charmian, Carolyn and her daughter Anna (from Guernsey) looked in for drinks. Anna is 16, a beautiful teen-ager, searching for what she should do after leaving school. She says she would like to read psychology and media studies. Her reading currently is Hello, and OK. Jenny noted she has beautiful teeth. I saw that she has lovely breasts and bare feet. Beware young fellahs. She will be a heart-breaker.

Today I phoned The Country Club at Quinta do Lago to enquire whether they were having much joy in attracting buyers for our October week. Angela said no. So I asked her to arrange for the week, our second week, to be rented out.

Wednesday ◆ JULY 23

A warm, still air. A carpet of dirty cloud. Families waiting for the longed for sun—soaked holiday. The national and international news is running down like sand in an hour glass as Parliamentarians disappear. It will be three months before they return to the Babel and babble of Westminster.

Locally, the asylum has a different look. On the metallic river, now a pond, startlingly white cruise liners eight storeys high steal slowly downstream as if exhausted. Below decks, down the curved, regal stairway you may walk through to a breakfast of difficult choices. Later, the pool, the Bar and the Follies in the Theatre with legs high-kicking, the Band blasting, and the stand-up seeking tired laughs in cracked and ageing faces.

For me, this morning, it is letters and coffee. Jenny is off to Pilates.

Thursday ◆ JULY 24

Jenny has arranged for the Minister, Brian, and his wife Mary to come for supper with David and Judy Mason in a week or so. Thus today I have been making 'place name cards' for the table and checked the quotations I require.

For Professor Sir David Mason I have chosen: 'What lies beneath the paving stones we cannot tell, but how will you lift those stones?' (MG) For Lady Judy Mason (who is Irish): Deep in the darkness pale hands so lovely carry a rich bunch of red roses for me.' (A song in a play by Sean O'Casey). For Minister Brian (who is also Irish): 'It is a love that I am seeking for, but of a beautiful, un-heard of kind that is not in the world.' (from The Shadowy Waters, By W.B. Yates). For the Minister's wife Mary: 'Love seeketh not itself to please, Nor for itself hath any care; But for another gives its ease And builds a Heaven in Hell's despair.' (Blake 1794).

For Jenny: 'God almighty first planted a garden; and, indeed, it is the purest of human pleasures.' (Francis Bacon 1561 – 1626). For myself: 'Well, I'll repent, and that suddenly, while I am in some liking; I shall be out of heart shortly, and then I shall have no strength to repent.' (Henry 1V, Part 1)

Friday ◆ JULY 25

With Marie at the wheel we arrived at the Academy in time to take champagne and encounter a crowd of unknown faces, all except for Hassie Young and Doris, Eric Stevenson's sister. With 100 other guests we then repaired to our table in the assembly hall where The Palm Court Trio was making a cheerful, twanging sound. We sat beneath silver balloons. On my left hand a well-dressed and nicely preserved lady (liking for bling) who was the wife of a church Minister opposite. On my right was an elderly lady with Alzheimers. She had a sweet smile but the ending of all the sentences she attempted to utter broke and fell into a void. Communication was very difficult. We sang Happy Birthday, Eric, and he made a long speech, most of which I could not hear. Before we left we were invited to take a copy of his book, enti-tled 'A kick out of Life.' I brought one home. It is an account of his life, from age 5, and seems to be well illustrated.

Saturday ◆ JULY 26

We worked hard all morning to prepare lunch for our neigh-bours, Peebles and Glens. I had already made plenty of soup, and we followed this with platters of fish of various kinds including a pyramid of pink prawns, smoked salmon and other Picean delicacies, with three different side salads, dressings, Marie Rose etc. There were strawberries, raspberries and nec-tarines, then cheeses and coffee. Gin and white wines flowed, as did the conversation which consisted mainly about golf and illness and houses. It was supposed to be a credit crunch lunch (' do not expect posh') but Jenny got over enthusiastic! Sheila and Jean talked us into the ground. Lunch ended when our guests left at 4.45 p.m. We then cleared up in time to leave for the golf club and join around 80 diners after drinks with Joyce and Alan Reid in their garden. Then, with Joyce and Alan at our table in the club were Geoffrey and Vivi Millar and the Mackintoshs. I think there were 10 tables going full blast and a great number of people I had never seen before hugging, kissing, exclaiming and laughing. A great demonstration of The Chattering Classes at play.

Sunday ◆ JULY 27

To Meeting, and Jenny to Hope Park Church. I was on door duty and post-worship coffee and biscuits duty. A quiet time with 14 quiet Friends. Jenny drove well through a thick Haar which lasted most of the day.

The East Glasgow election demolishment of Labour fills the news. There are calls for Prime Minister Brown to stand down.

The Bishops, meeting in York, are still stupidly divided over issues concerning the acceptance of women Bishops and homosexual clergy. Many consider The Anglican Communion to be, as it were, lost in the Haar.

Monday ◆ JULY 28

Ach, alas! The haar is still down. A grey, clammy nothingness. Silence. Just the electricity in your grey matter buzzing. Where has the world gone?

From Istanbul came a lesson on how to bomb, maim and kill ordinary folk. It happened in a poor suburb. First, a small bomb to get the populace running to the scene. Then a much bigger bomb to slaughter them.

It's not unusual. Try to be cheerful. Or is it manic laughter that I hear? The days of wine and roses are short-lived. The days of violence and grief are ever present. Very obviously this is the year of the bomb, the knife and the greedy Banks.

Tuesday ◈ **JULY 29**

In Heavens name, what next in this Year of Disgrace? We know all about Labour wanting to 'get rid' of PM Brown, but do we really know about those Bishops of the C of E now accused of abusing their wives? But, the saddest news story concerns a lady doctor on her honeymoon in idyllic Antigua. She was shot dead in the head and her husband was shot in the neck.

More misery? China, gearing up for the Olympics, is again being accused of infringing human rights. Could be true.

This morning I sent an e-mail to Eric Stevenson. I have read half of his book, and in his chapter called 'Oh What a Lovely War' I noted that he was just ahead of my unit on the long haul to Hamburg in World War 11. His tank group captured and destroyed Venlo. We followed in with our ambulances the day after, and set about picking up the dead, the dying and the homeless. I never knew Eric was in tanks, nor did he know that I was hard on his heels.

Wednesday ◈ **JULY 30**

The world seemed to be smaller in the second part of Eric's book, and much of the post-war detail was trivia, especially the playtime with speed boats The Chamber of Commerce story was more interesting. I was amused by the account of his time as a Holyrood Constable. Not so long ago I encountered the Constables at Holyrood in their quaint blue uniforms. The Band had been asked to play in the Long Room for a Royal visit. We were instructed to strike up when the Royal (Princess Alexandra) entered. We asked a Constable what he suggested we should play. He went to enquire and on returning said "She would like you to play Love is the Sweetest Thing." So we did, and then played on as the formalities got under way.

Today Jenny is off to the golf club and to Pilates, and this evening will go with the girls to see Mama Mia (the film) in St. Andrews.

Thursday ◆ JULY 31

Surely there must be some good news. And there is! Dossie is to have her second baby, and Clare has recently delivered her first, and Verity Marr is nursing her second. That is good cheer. Globally, as of this minute, many millions are in bed together, or coupling in taxis, back bedrooms. front parlours, behind the Speakers' Chair in The Commons, on commons or under trees and absolutely everywhere so, accidentally or not, there will be millions more babies being made right now! Meanwhile, today, there are millions of aged folk tottering into their nineties. The Anglican Communion is still quarrelling about homosexuality. And an incredible number of people of all ages and nationalities are taking drugs, committing adultery and murder, stealing, shooting, bombing and cutting down valuable rain forests. Happily, there are at least some folk saying their prayers and attending Mothers' Circle and doing sewing meetings, and raising money for a vast swathe of international charities. C'est la vie in the asylum.

Millie kept us awake last night. She was sick twice and is unwell this morning. We have to take two chairs to Cupar to be recovered. But wait. Jenny has just reported that Millie is still being sick. We will take her to the Vet. After an examination the Vet said they would do X-rays. Later, he reported that they would keep Millie in overnight, but hoped she would not need another operation.

Friday ◆ AUGUST 1

GUESTS FROM GRANADA

We phoned the Vet. They have decided to keep Millie in today. She will be given some food, and we hope she will keep it down.

It is still raining stair rods. Not to be deterred, Jenny is going out to play in the Ladies' shotgun foursome. It poured all night throughout Britain. We are becoming a rain-sodden island.

Again, we rang the Vet. The report was not favourable, but we were told we could bring Millie home and see how she managed. She lay still and was clearly miserable and suffering.

Saturday ◆ AUGUST 2

Last night turned upside down. I had no sleep as Millie climbed on and off our bed then stood staring vacantly into the darkened hall. I think she was in pain. This morning I am exhausted. Poor Millie, she would not eat the tinned diet the Vet had sold us. She simply sat on the window seat, and after dribbling drank some water and was then dreadfully sick. We rang the Vat at nine and will have to take her back. Gemma is upset and barking, clearly reacting to Millie's plight. Vet Steve Clark took her in and gave us a very thorough report. He will keep Millie overnight, and depending on her condition tomorrow morning he will decide whether Millie will have to go under the knife again. I am very sad. The only cheer was to hear, and see, that wonderful pro-gramme 'Last Choir Standing.' It just gave me heart. The sheer joy of those competitors was deeply moving.

Sunday ◆ AUGUST 3

As we feared, Millie will have an op. this morning. We will get the result around noon. Later when Steve Clark rang he said they found a foreign object in Millie's bowel. He will keep it to show us. It sounds to me like something someone has thrown out from one of the many barbecues that happen on the dunes and beach which is where Millie is daily taken on her walk. She will be kept at the surgery until Wednesday or Thursday when, all being well, she can come home. Poor Mills. She will be sore, but we are relieved that the surgeon found nothing more sinister.

Monday ◆ AUGUST 4

More phone calls. Millie is suffering. Morphine to the rescue. We keep in touch.

Tuesday ◆ AUGUST 5

We are busy preparing supper for tonight. It is the one we planned a while back for Prof. David Mason and Judy, with Minister

Brian and his wife Mary. We will offer smoked salmon, prawns and melon, followed by Jenny's ham with Cumberland sauce and lots of veg, then seasonal fruits, cheeses and coffee.

News: In the Holy Land Israel is now creating small Jewish settlements in Palestinian territory. Again. A while back I wrote to Ming Campbell about that big fence that Israel has illegally erected. Ming raised the matter with the (then) Foreign Sec. Jack Straw. He responded to Ming as follows: "I share your constituents' concern about the grave situation in the Middle East. The UK Government remains fully committed to the roadmap and continues to work towards the vision of a two-state solution.

Israel has the right to take steps, within international law, to protect itself from terrorist attack. But lasting security can only be delivered by a negotiated settlement. The construction of the fence on occupied territory can only harm the prospects for peace. The demolition and confiscation of Palestinian land associated with the construction of the fence is unlawful and creates a physical obstacle to the two-state solution. Tony Blair and I expressed our concerns about its route to the Israeli Prime Minister, Ariel Sharon, on his visit to London on 14 July. Baroness Symons reiterated this when she met the Israeli Foreign Minister, Silvan Shalom in Israel on 30 September, and did so again on her recent visit to the occupied territories. We continue to make representations to the Israeli authorities at official level at London and through our Embassy and Consulate General in Tel Aviv and Jerusalem. "

Alas, the fence is still there, a barrier to lasting peace.

The cheerful news today is that two people got married at 1,000 ft above Cirencester, strapped to the wings of two by-planes flying at 100 m.p.h with the Minister standing on the wings of a third plane. Many mortals get the wind up before they wed, but this, for the intrepid bride and groom, was just a breeze!

David and Judy and Brian and Mary blew in on time for supper. They had not met before but seemed happy in each others company. Minister Brian is a cheerful man with a fund of good stories, and David liked this very much.

Wednesday ◈ AUGUST 6

The Vet reports that Millie is doing well. She is not eating much yet but could come home tomorrow. It should help her recovery.

Thursday ◈ AUGUST 7

Some one, somewhere, has decided that we should have bad news and unending tales of woe. This morning Dorothy Dickson rang to tell us that her eldest daughter (Caroline is in her early Thirties) has been diagnosed as having MS. She is a cheery, attractive and successful girl. We all love her. The family seems to suffer ill-luck. Michael is still ill but somehow survives; Dorothy (wife) is still unable to drive a car as her foot is still to heal. For Heaven's sake, what next?

Will the new English cricket captain Kevin Pieterson get his team out today to play the final Test on a damp pitch or will they have to hang about in the locker room nibbling apples until the rain ceases?

No! It was actually sunny at The Oval. Pieterson's side bowled S. Africa out for 194.

We have just brought a very quiet, subdued Millie back home. The Vet gave us the object she had swallowed. It was a one and half inches chunk of thick, partly burned wood.

Friday ◈ AUGUST 8

Last evening Alison Chapman, up from Sussex for a family holiday, looked in for supper. She said she liked Thai food, so I did the business and we all enjoyed it. Alison grew up in Earlsferry and has always loved this coast. She is excellent company.

Gemma is behaving beautifully with an invalid Millie.

This morning Elizabeth Marr is calling in for lunch with daughter Katy, son– in– law Colin Hart, and their child Alex. They have come up from The Borders to visit the Pittenweem Arts Festival.

Saturday ◆ AUGUST 9

It was a good lunch yesterday and a pleasure to see Colin again, and his son Alex (aged 3) and marvellous Mum, Katy who will have her second child in February. Together they turned back a small curtain in the asylum to show a natural, binding love and tenderness together.

Yesterday we also had an explosion of joy, colour and general happiness as The Olympic Games in China opened up in the largest, blazing pyrotechnic display ever seen by Man. The other explosions were less friendly as Russia and Georgia set about bombing and shelling each other.

Sunday ◆ AUGUST 10

Managed to get to Meeting despite flooding and roads closed. This made us late on returning for the drinks party given by Stella and Graham Harvey. They have rented holiday house by the beach. The sun appeared so we mingled in the garden. Later, I saw on TV that The PGA Masters in Michigan was won by Harrington with Garcia as runner up. Podraig has now won three Masters back-to-back. A superb achievement.

Monday ◆ August 11

Dangerous days in Georgia as the bloody battle with Russian forces continues in a tangled and complex political mess. When will the talking begin? Politics, prejudice, territorial ambition, the lust for power, possessions and domination continue unabated. There is an urgent need for all parties to halt the violence, and engage in intelligent discourse. Those angry adversaries are simply visitors, tenants on the planet. The Earth is not theirs to own, and their time here is strictly limited. Can they not appreciate what they have got? After two world wars, plus Iraq, The Middle East, Africa, Afghanistan, widespread poverty and the failing Western democracies, we appear to have learned nothing.

Tuesday ◈ AUGUST 12

Another rainy day. So, down the Pub. I view the ritual. A regular was standing at the Bar. "Pint 'a' Special." Fumble for your change. Stand erect. Watch motionless as the Barman pulls and fills. There it is. The tall, plain pint glass. Clear amber to the white collar at the brim. A column of gold speaking eloquently to your thirst. Wait. Don't touch. Stand erect. Stand and wait. Observe the coming pleasure.

"You got nuts ?"

"Yes man. Salt or roasted?"

"Salt." A fumble for more change. Then, reach for it and grasp the golden pillar. One good sip. Then stand back. Observe. The tall tube of gold. Wait. Then another taste and stand tall, like the Special. You are special. And normal, like millions in jeans and unremarkable shirts. Stand and watch. Open the nuts. Get a few in the palm of your hand and throw them, head back, into your mouth. Crunch and the bits get stuck between your teeth. But, you're okay. Upright. Like the gold before you. No hurry. Take your time. Another sip. The world's, yes, okay. That's until you get back home. And TV. In Georgia 130 Russian tanks. Many civilians killed. Too many. And 10,000 displaced persons. So, there is talk of a ceasefire. Can it happen?

Wednesday ◈ AUGUST 13

Blame Bush, not the American people. They are busy losing their homes or trying to raise a mortgage. It's Bush. Too eager to bring Georgia on side as part of a Western Democracy. And get the oil of course, as in Iraq. Oily Bush, goodbye. Stop meddling. And, Mister Brown, Southwold is lovely, but come home now. Holidays are over, and Summer never started anyway. Season of mists and fruitfulness is at hand. But fruitful is difficult. Talk to a farmer about harvest and you'll not get a reply. He is too busy prizing his machinery out of the mud.

Thursday ◆ AUGUST 14

Yesterday's words sound a tad gloomy. But, Hell's Bells, can anyone assure me that there are no options except gloom and doom. Those demons get us nowhere. There are thinking people, I am sure, who strive not to be depressed. No point. Do your best to be alive. Today I am going to make courgette and mint soup. Well, I HAVE TO. Sheila from next door keeps hanging courgette on our garden fence. It is clear that in the asylum there are all shades of colours as well as shadows. One of the darkest is that there are more than one billion people living in slums, many of them in India. One billion is a hefty percentage of the total population living in the asylum.

Friday ◆ AUGUST 15

The sun called by with brilliance and tempting heat, and at noon bade me test the humidity by driving down the Pub for that swift half. Hoards of visitors did the same. Families. Dogs. Push chairs and the familiar obese, ugly, ill-clad, a selection of humanity gloomily looking for the holiday they never had (schools go back in a couple of days). The sun had an hour's holiday. Then the cumulus gathered overhead. Black clouds inked out the blue bits and the temperature dropped like an over-ripe apple from the bough. That's your summer hols for you. Jenny is testing herself on the links and will then be in the club until six. I'll go spin the soup. And take a bath.

Saturday ◆ AUGUST 16

News: The Russian occupation of large areas of Georgia is causing more international concern and the media is talking of another "Cold War." Russia versus the United States of America. They should pipe down, there is enough hot war around as it is. The White House is intent on putting missile shields in Poland fronting Russia who is understandably disturbed. Some mad politicians are even talking of "a nuclear strike." This simply adds to the existing lunacy in the asylum. Nation versus nation, and everyone feeling threatened.

It is the Olympics that can refresh us. A wee girl from England has swum her way into two golds. She is very excited. She said "I worked very, very hard to win." Her name is Rebecca Adlington. Adding to British success also was gold for our coxless four. And our cycling heroes. And tonight I found more joy in Last Choir Standing.

Sunday ◆ AUGUST 17

Isla Charlotte Ross Johnson is just six months old, and today she went to church. She is Clare's beautiful child, the latest addition to the Dickson clan, and was there to be christened. Some 50 of the family attended, mothers, sisters, cousins, aunts, uncles, Nanny, friends young and old the world and his wife, including us. The church was packed. Jenny was on the door, and also had to read Psalm 100 (verses 1 - 5). In her own terms she spoke with a kind of solemn joy. There were six hymns plus the address to the children and the sermon – "The rare jewel of Christian contentment."

So, it was a case of stand up, sit down, then keep standing up and sitting down for an hour or so. Up and down. It is a curious ritual for a Quaker, with little time for quiet, actual worship. I was troubled by the concept of contentment. My own belief is that true Christian Faith is not an all is well affair. It is a tough and rocky road. No matter. That is how it is for The Church of Scotland. And, of course, for Isla, the child beautiful in the safe arms of the Minister. Afterwards we were invited to join the family at Cadgers Way for lunch. Champagne. wonderful food, and a time for the warmth of love, and fellowship.

Monday ◆ AUGUST 18

Multi-cultural Britain may not have much of a Government but it has developed a new and agreeable shine, thanks to Beijing. We accolade our athletes. So far: 36 medals! Chico Ramos and Kathy drove over for our annual crab lunch today. To make a start on a Continental footing I devised Miguel's Silver Tapas Bar which contained roasted nuts, jumbo prawns with Marie Rose, sliced chourico, gherkins, and small rolls of salami stuffed with Isle of

Mull cheddar. Kathy brought olives and a bottle of Burgundy while I supplied Vinho Verde and Palmela. Chico did the business with the crabs which followed my courgette and mint soup and, to finish, we had a plate of sliced melon. We ate in The Bird Cage, but could not enjoy the wonderful view it affords, as the rain fell ceaselessly throughout the day. The only sunshine we saw was in some 50 photographs that Chico had taken on their recent three weeks in Viana do Castelo.

News: Pakistan's President Musharraf has resigned after nine years of misrule. More concern in a troubled land with 'nuclear capability.'In Georgia the Russian militia refuses to retreat after the signing of a cease-fire agreement. (They will do as they do do, and there's no doing anything about it).

Tuesday ◆ AUGUST 19

Britain's Gold Medals shine on as our' Foreign Minister does his PR bit with the President of Georgia. This talk is pretty useless. Russia does not care one Vodka cocktail whether Britain loves Georgia or not. The scenario is simple. Russia does not want the West (ie Nato allies) camped on her borders and thus be capable of planting arms there; but the West wants to be in those neighbouring states for defence, and for economic and political reasons. It is a stupid situation.

Wednesday ◆ AUGUST 20

Disaster. True, this is the wettest August since records began. But that is not the disaster, Shortly after lunch today a Spanair aircraft, with around 170 people on board crashed on take off at Madrid and went up in flames. The port side engine caught fire. Fifty ambulances went to the scene of the crash and four of Madrid's hospitals were alerted. It is thought that maybe 20 passengers survived, injured. Few of them are likely to live.

Thursday ◆ AUGUST 21

Olympic success apart there can be no denying that 2008 is a terrible year. Three days of mourning for those passengers killed.

Cause of the disaster not yet declared. Was the port engine on fire at take off? Was there an element of pilot error? How far was mechanical failure to blame? At V1 the Captain and/or the First Officer can abort on the runway. At V2 (shortly before "rotate") maybe not. But sadly, whatever the cause there is nothing that can console those hundreds of families so sorely devastated. Their families and friends died in a hell of flames.

This morning Jenny has gone to see Dr. Wilson. She has been experiencing bouts of dizziness. Answer: pills given, blood taken, X-ray of cervicals arranged. Tomorrow we leave for Aboyne with our dogs and prepare for Saturday's gig.

Friday ◆ AUGUST 22

I wish I could subdue the flesh that sorely troubles me (Betjeman I think). Well, I salute it The flesh I mean. There were 150 lovely young women in ball gowns with bare shoulders and backs, exhibiting pale, soft, smooth skin. And it shone, it flashed across the wide floor of the Coo Cathedral, as with their consorts those maidens danced the night down until four a.m. (The cathedral is a former byre). But, I get ahead of myself. That was Saturday, this is Friday. With 10 pieces of (drum) kit, two dogs, and changes of clothes, we drove up to Lys-na- Greyne House at Aboyne, Dee-side. Meg and David, as ever, made us welcome with tea and shortbread, and we made them happy when they were introduced to Gemma whom they brought into the world. I promised they should see how she was developing. They thought she was brilliant, "just like her mum!" After unpacking in the big, wide-windowed bedroom overlooking the Dee we took the dogs to Mo Fettes at Crathes and later had supper at The Candlestick Maker.

Saturday ◆ AUGUST 23

After breakfast we set up the drums in Coo Cathedral, then had a bowl of soup for lunch at Colonel Rose's wee restaurant (and shop) at Finzean (pron. Fingan). We ate outside under a blue sky, then returned to Aboyne where I climbed into bed and stayed there until 6.00 p.m. to get up steam for the inevitably tiring six and a half hour non-stop stint with the Band. Before the off Meg gave us a super dinner with pheasant. Earlier, in the sitting room we had canape and too much wine. Then, the beauty, the wild dancing, the Ball gowns and bling, a flurry of white tie and tails, kilts, scarlet mess jackets, and even naval two-ringers. In all 320 noisy, cheery dancers crowded the floor. Each one had paid £80.00 to dance to our music which included reels, jigs, jazz, rock 'n' roll, Latino, everything in the chattering classes book. There was breakfast with smoked salmon, eggs, sausages, cheese et al, including wine, coffee or tea or orange juice from 2.00 a.m. Andy and Nicky Bradford (of Interval Band days) gave us a brief break with Nelly the Elephant etc. I found my bed at 4.45 a.m. but was too weary (and sore) to attempt even four hours' sleep. Then, after a cooked breakfast, we collected and packed the kit, then picked up Millie and Gemma at Crathes, and took the long road back to Fife.

Sunday ◆ AUGUST 24

We called at Harvey McGuires again for a light lunch before reaching home and slumping. Distantly, on TV, I heard that Britain's athletes were leaving Beijing in triumph with 47 medals. (19 were Gold). The London Games in 2012 will cost £9 billion. The Chinese event, now ended with flags, dancing and another pyrotechnic blaze, was planned over 10 years. A spend of a cool £20 billion.

Monday ◆ AUGUST 25

In yesterday's Sunday Times Culture magazine, Bryan Appleyard displayed the items he would put in his personal time capsule. And he suggested readers might care to say what personal item they would put in theirs. I replied that I would put this Journal in. Jenny said she would put in a bicycle pump, or a golf bag with putter, or a laptop.

Tuesday ◆ AUGUST 26

Jenny had an X-Ray of her cervicals. I had a massage. Then all the usual chores. Also hired a Prince Charlie for the forthcoming wedding of Olivia (Holly) and Manolo in Edinburgh on Saturday.

Wednesday ◈ AUGUST 27

Spent the night driving from Washington to Nashville, Tennessee. My courteous host and hostess offered me champagne. In reality that would have been a very long drive. But, why go there? It would also be a long, long drive to Denver, Colorado where the Democrats are having their big, jazzy convention. It will introduce Jo Biden (Obama's running mate). Hilary Clinton made a brilliant, impassioned speech telling all present to support Obama or else there could be a dreaded four years of McCain as a clone of Bush. That is the reality. In the above dream my hosts showed me a broken down clapboard shack selling candy and jello. In black ink above the lintel was one word. Bush.

Thursday ◈ AUGUST 28

The Colarado Dem's convention, in a storm of joy, has officially elected Obama as their candidate for Pres. Meantime Russia and the US continue to play political chess, with our Foreign Secretary helping to push the pawns around the board. He's in the Ukraine making speeches, telling Russia not to start a Cold War. It is time our political goons stopped thinking and talking war. It is time to find some trust. It is time to sit around one big table, extend a hand and start talking peace and sensible economic co-operation. Then doing it.

Friday ◈ AUGUST 29

A ripple of a white horse under cloudless blue. A warm breath from the south east, and a 21 footer under main and jib nods its way slowly upstream. So has summer really arrived at last? I sit. waiting, feet on the wall, a Belhaven before me above a full tide. I feel I am a lone figure, smart in a brass-buttoned blazer. I am lonely. Maybe others are too. I am thinking of India, and the vast floods in the north. Millions homeless and no clean water.

Here, on the greens the ladies, with Jenny, bend over their putts. It is blazingly hot. Good for cricket. At the Oval, England after 40 overs are 296 for 7. South Africa will again be beaten and lose the series.

Tomorrow Holly weds Manolo in Edinburgh and we play for the dancing.

Saturday ◆ AUGUST 30

After Jenny had taken Millie and Gemma to the kennels we piled into the car with clothes and my kit. Edinburgh was like an ant hill, swarming with walkers, as vast crowds flooded pavements the last of the back-packing Festival thousands. We man-handled the kit to the top floor of The New Club in Princes Street and un-packed drums cymbals, stands et al, then sought lunch. We found it in La Petite Folie. (I had good mussels in a tomato soup and excellent poulet).

Then back to change, and a cab down to the church in Canon-gate. Jenny was svelt, lovely. Big black chapeau. Guests gather-ing. Swarming. Kissing. Manolo's family and friends mingled, cameras flashing. In the cool church the whispered ceremony took place with good hymns which the guests from Granada could not sing, and the Scots and Angle Saxons did no better. Holly looked happy, smiling, assured, with a confident Manolo. We then all packed into waiting coaches as the bride and groom swooshed away in a golden Rolls Royce.

In the club we drank champagne, or white wine or chilled beer, and sampled canape including Spicy Haggis Parcels, Gress-ingham Duck on Brioche with Sweet Chile Sauce, Marinaded Prawns in a Pastry Case, Roast Salmon Skewers with Lime, Coriander & Maple Honey, Toasted Rosemary and Garlic Focca-cia with Humous, Pork and Herb Cocktail Sausages, Iberian Bel-lota Ham from Guijuelo, Salamanca, Iberian Bellota Chorizo from Guijuelo Salamanca, a Selection of Manchego Cheeses Maese Miguel (Ciadad Real) and Vega de Sotuelamos (Albacete).

And then Dinner, with Timbale of Hot Smoked Salmon with a Watercress and Lemon Crème Fraiche followed by Scottish Beef with a Red Wine and Challot Jus, Grilled Tomatoes, Chateau Potatoes and Asparagus. The pud was Wedding Cake with Seasonal Scottish berries and cream. We drank a Club Sauv Blanc, Chateau La Grand Maye 2005, and coffee. Nicky did his College Grace from Cambridge in Latin; Rachel made a short oration in Spanish, and Euan had us raising our glasses to Holly and Manolo as the citizens of Granada roared some special incantation! Jenny and I sat on The Bride's Mother's table (La Gran Taberna) with Robin and Patti Bell and a most attractive French woman (aged 50 ?) who had some connection with the Cannes festival and fairly glittered with French charm. I could not eat the Scottish beef, but that Bellota Ham one could live for ever on that I then changed in our room and raced down to my kit and the dance was on. Presents? The 'Home' ladies received Spanish pottery and the ladies from Grenada had pottery from Crail. For chaps, whisky. Our present to bride and groom was a silver quaich.

After the Band, the Disco. I sat out on the balcony with Jenny and Euan until 1.00.m., and around us in lazy conversation was Granada –- Paco, Rosario, Pilar, Maria del Mar, Carmen, Jose Manuel, Fernando, Alicio, and all the others, whispering, disco dancing, admiring and being happy. Holly is now Mrs Manolo Frias Valdiva.

Sunday ◈ AUGUST 31

Having slept the remaining dark hours in the club we had breakfast with Euan then packed the car with clothes and kit and drove across town for coffee with Chico and Kathy who kindly gave me a present of coffee beans from Portugal. Then, it was back to Fife and the kennels to pick up the dogs.

Monday ◈ SEPTEMBER 1

THE BIG BANG

Some necessary multi-shopping in St. Andrews. Then we asked David and Sheila to call in for pre-dinner drinks. We talked 'parish pump.'

NEWS: Hurricanes hitting Louisiana coast; the flooding in Behar (NE India) is a national disaster, with figures, probably inaccurate, of the homeless now given as between one and three million; The Shropshire home of the millionaire that was fired (arson) now reveals the bodies of him, her, and daughter. All shot in the head before being burned; Man United and Man City have each bought a star player at £30 million a skull. Money seems to have entered a different universe. The winner of the National Lottery on Saturday will be £90 million richer.

Tuesday ◆ SEPTEMBER 2

Bought scallops. Took Jenny and the dogs down the Pub because the sun was bright and hot and all the canvas–knickered tourists had fled back to offices, to interminable family meals, the usual rows, exhaustion, the Telly and school runs.

Wednesday ◆ SEPTEMBER 3

This morning, on looking up to vast continents of banked, grey clouds I felt the globe turning, and a sense of change. Everywhere. But then, I checked my Journal for the year 2002 and on this date (3rd) found the following: – 'There would appear to be delay and prevarication in Jo'burg at the World Summit on Sustainable Development. What a deplorable mess, with civil servants and political leaders from everywhere living in five-star hotels and eating in five-star restaurants, while down the road in the shanty towns poverty casts its shadow, ensuring early death through disease and near starvation. An obscene and grossly insensitive situation. It would not be so bad if the countries represented at the Summit could agree on renewable energy but no! America, the oil kingdoms and many Arab nations simply do not want it. Will anything remotely sensible or compassionate result from this meeting of African and European minds? Meanwhile, warships and aircraft are setting their own agenda, moving through the Med and into The Gulf, perhaps to take up battle stations for a pre-emptive strike.'

Thursday ◆ SEPTEMBER 4

Sarah Palin, the Governor from Alaska, is determined to make a constructive difference to the Republican's campaign for The

White House. McCain has chosen her as his running mate and, according to the media, she is a popular choice – even if she has a 17 year old daughter who is pregnant, and herself possesses limited political experience.

Meantime Mother Earth does her own thing. It is confirmed that the flooding in Behar has left 3 million homeless, without clean water, and with little or no food, not just for a day but for weeks. It is the worst flooding experienced on the Indian continent for 80 years. And there is more. The Polar icecap has set free an immense carpet of ice (not just a wee iceberg). There is a lot of talk about global warming.

Yesterday afternoon I found a descendent of George 1V over here to cut her lawn. She was on her own so I said "Would you care to come and have supper with us?" She came, and we burned the candles down as we put the world to rights. She is Sheila Gordon, wife of Peter Gordon (Dr. retired). She does valuable work for Riding for The Disabled.

Friday ◆ SEPTEMBER 5

The phone hardly ceased ringing yesterday, there were e-mails to write and e-mails to receive, as well as letters, bills, insurance worries, ironing, cooking and all the bits and pieces of the daily jig-saw that have to be fitted together. The downturn in the economy is biting, and today the media is reporting the continuing angst about the steep rises in the cost of gas and electricity which is already hitting poorer or disadvantaged families and, of course, many pensioners. Back benchers at Westminster are imploring Prime Minister Brown to help poorer households cope with energy bills. The energy companies, with their vast profits, are also coming in for a public roasting because they too, so far, are refusing to play Robin Hood, and help the needy. The Government line is "insulate your loft, see to your cavity wall insulation, and fit the dim light bulbs – that way you will save on heating bills." The problem is that there are plenty of families that have done all of that and STILL can't pay their bills. All right, cut down on holidays, stop the booze and fags, don't borrow — and don't do Christmas presents, not even for the kids. Don't weep or worry. Try to smile.

Saturday ◆ SEPTEMBER 6

Noel Coward used to sing "There are bad times just around the corner", and he was right! But the situation is not hopeless, as Prof. Sandy said in his tutorial on the world of Finance when we called to purchase some decent red in his Wine Gallery. He reflected on the fat cats who earn (and keep) obscene amounts of money and widen the gap between the haves and the have nots. And he agreed with me that the media does not help matters as they scare the public with stories of doom and gloom. (As a former media person, that makes me feel guilty now). Even so, this sensible, elderly man refused to be down hearted.

Well, I'll have to cook the sausages tonight, as Jenny is out with Les Girls for a Pub supper. It is the golf club's AGM and the men's black tie dinner. I used to go to it each year, leading the band and the marching to the club. But I found the dinner and the none too clever speeches rather boring.

Sunday ◆ SEPTEMBER 7

A very small Quaker Meeting today, but I was charmed to meet a delightful young woman who, it turned out, had attended St. Leonards school for girls from "well-to-do" families, the same institution in which Jenny was incarcerated throughout her formative years. When Martha Hamilton was Headmistress she used to take her senior girls to the Himalayas. Today such expeditions may incur greater risk. For example, Cuba and Haiti are currently off limits. Yet another hurricane is destroying thousands of homes there and will no doubt threaten the South American coastline. England is becoming more waterlogged with serious flooding. This time it is the town of Morpeth that is worst hit, with many homes evacuated, and there are flood warnings over wide areas in the south west. A lot of baling out, which is echoed at a different level in the USA. The two massive mortgage lenders dealing in trillions of dollars (Fannie Mae and Freddie Mac) have gone bust and are having to be baled out by the Government. To add to the general joy the Civil Service unions here may go on strike for better pay. Thousands of their members are among the lowest paid workers in the country. And that is wrong.

But, there is good news. Andrew Murray has put world Number One Nadal to bed 3 sets to one, and tomorrow in the US Open final will attempt to do the same to Federer.

Monday ◈ SEPTEMBER 8

Joseph had a technicolour dream coat. I think we all have one and the colours are brightest when we are in our prime our rainbow time. As we grow older the colours begin to fade, and if we grow really ancient they become as grey as an asphalt puddle of water. (I'm beginning to get my feet wet).

Tuesday ◈ SEPTEMBER 9

Yesterday Andrew Murray became a little older. Federer, playing the best tennis of his career, despatched him 6 - 2, 7 - 5, 6 - 2 in little more than two hours. Nevertheless, Murray did win five out of six of his US Open matches and came away with head held high – and at least one million dollars in his pocket.

Wednesday ◈ SEPTEMBER 10

There might be an amused smile on the face of God today. It is Big Bang Day. The particle accelerator goes into action underground in Switzerland as excited physicists stand by to measure, among other things, mass, and learn secrets which, they hope, will reveal the state of the universe seconds after God's Bang. This is all brilliant science, but I imagine God saying "Okay, boys and girls, go right ahead. Have a try, but don't get big ideas. It is my intention to preserve certain secrets to myself and will not share them with you. So – watch it!"

As the particles whizz about we at home are still trying to sort out masses of paper and old files. Jenny has just handed me a couple of her school reports when she was six years and two months old. English and needlework were tops, marked "very good indeed." Numbers and physical training were excellent as was conduct: "Thoughtful and kind." Singing, alas, was only very fair. Scripture "Is not a good listener and does not answer questions." In geography she was also not good at answering questions.

Thursday ◆ SEPTEMBER 11

Ground Zero in NY. They assembled in what looked like a vast builders' yard, young, old, middle aged, some carrying poster-like photos of loved ones who had died there. It was the seventh anniversary of 9/11. There was silence. No cause for sentimentality. We all know of a friend, or a friend of a friend who died when the two planes drove headlong into the towers.

At that moment Jenny and I were ten miles from Glasgow, en route to leave our car in Alan Mackie's drive before he would kindly drive us to the airport. Ten miles to go and I phoned Alan for a precise direction to his home and was astonished when he simply said "It's war." We had not heard the news. Our plan had been to fly Glasgow to Heathrow and thence to Porto (Portugal) where Chico would meet us and take us to Viana de Castelo for a joint holiday with him and his family. Alan told us the terrible news as he drove us to the airport. We checked with BA. Heathrow was blocked with passengers aiming to get to NY. They were sleeping on the floor in their thousands. It was no go. We returned to our car and a week or so later found a direct flight to Faro. Chico and Kathy drove down from Viana and were with us for a week. It was a kind of holiday, but despite sunshine and golf there were not so many smiles.

Friday ◆ SEPTEMBER 12

Will it be Obama or McCain who will build again on Ground Zero? McCain's secret weapon, Sarah Palin, appears to be tilting voting preference in favour of the Republicans. Yesterday we decided to purchase a fridge-freezer to replace the large 'box' freezer we have had for years. Jenny set to work to create some space. She did a marvellous job, although she was not happy to dispose of the big freezer. I attended to other household chores and now have completed three soups. The biggest daily bore is the mass of junk mail. Why do so many Psychic Healers' attack me? Today, one who says she is world famous writes: "Michael, we have not met yet but I feel you and I have a special bond We can communicate on a higher level than the physical sense. Let me explain." She says she is off to Lourdes to pray for me, and to resolve a problem with my wife, and my children. She seeks to bring love into my life, to improve my health, to have luck on the lottery or in the casino. What nonsense!

Saturday ◈ SEPTEMBER 13

This terrible year in the asylum is in desperate need of laughter, or at least some cheery news. It is hard to find. The Channel tunnel has been closed for two days due to fire, leaving many thousands of travellers stuck at either end. The XL travel agency has collapsed leaving very many more travellers stranded around the world and 1700 staff jobless. As the result of hurricanes much of Haiti has been destroyed with hundreds of thousands homeless and in need of water, food and medicines. A national emergency. One million people have been told to flee the Texas and the Louisiana coast as hurricane Ike makes landfall and hits Galvaston. Vast areas flooded and homes destroyed. In New York there is near panic as the fat cats strive to save the possible collapse of the influential Lehman Brothers Bank which controls assets of $600 billion.

It is back to Beijing to find a note of cheer. In the paraplegic Olympic games Britain is lying second to China and continuing to win gold. One of the most heartening sights of the year so far is to witness those athletes overcoming incredible disadvantage and accepting their accolades with delight and a moving dignity.

Sunday ◈ SEPTEMBER 14

I said to Jenny "Those five pans, why don't we use them in the kitchen and throw the old frying pans out?

"Because I want to keep them," she replied.

"But we don't need both lots. And these five are much better, they're copper with brass handles, and they are lined with silver."

"I know. Father William got them from the chef at Grosvenor House in Park Lane."

"So what?

"I like them. They make me think of Father William."

"You mean, every time you use a frying pan you think of Father William?

"Yes, of course."

"But couldn't you think of your father without resorting to the pans ?"

"I'd like to keep them, but I might give them to Peter." (her nephew).

"Good ! So – let's do it! "

"Not now. I want to think about it.

"Okay! Tomorrow, then. Next week?

"NO! I'll think about it."

Not good, said a little voice back of my head. You'll just have to live in a house with at least ten frying pans when there is only ever a need for four, (not counting the 12 other pans in the kitchen).

Monday ◆ **SEPTEMBER 15**

The Big Bang Boys at Cern in Switzerland continue to accelerate their particles to learn more about our universe, but another big bang has just occurred in New York where, as feared, Lehman Brothers has filed for bankruptcy, and Merrill Lynch is being saved (bought) by The Bank of America. The tremors from those vast financial institutions are felt all round the world with more Banks, and businesses at risk. But, there is some cheering news. On Friday at Valhalla in Kentucky the Ryder Cup will provide three days of oohs and aahs.

I will be glued to the TV. Meantime I will keep an eye on my tender balance at The Clydesdale Bank. There are, of course, wealthy folk, like Sir Richard Branson who do not have to count their bawbees. When asked how to become a millionaire he said it was simple. "Start out as a billionaire, then launch an airline!"

Tuesday ❖ SEPTEMBER 16

The Scottish National Portrait Gallery is one of the ugliest buildings in town, but the portrait photographs (1913 - 2008) currently on view there are superb. They are all from Vanity Fair which, after a decade, re-established itself in 1983. A feast of faces and bodies including celebs like Monet, Hockney, Madonna and a great number of Hollywood luminaries from Chaplin to Garbo. The brilliant photographers included Cecil Beaton, Man Ray, Baron de Meyer, Annie Leibovitz, and Mario Testino. With Chico and Kathy we stared and rejoiced for two hours before eating lunch at La Petite Folie in Frederick Street. Big bowls of moules. Those famous faces told history, so we had a day of relief from the news of financial disasters and the grotesque grumbling and posturing in the Labour Party.

Wednesday ❖ SEPTEMBER 17

Shopping, soup making, and a harness for Gemma so that she does not pull Jenny's shoulder to bits during her morning walk.

Thursday ❖ SEPTEMBER 18

We visited that wonderful shop opposite the fish market in Pittenweem. FMA (Fishermens' Mutual Association) because Jenny required a new pair of welly boots. They sell everything that a modest house or a costly trawler might require, from tin tacks and teacups to woollies and shirts. It's a true fishy bazaar.

Friday ❖ SEPTEMBER 19

Last night on TV we watched the opening of the Ryder Cup. Massive parades of Kentucky Bands, and speeches. The American presenter, mike in hand, was brilliant, but captains Nick Faldo and Azinger, introducing their teams were dreadful. Not one jot of humour.

Bouncing back is the name of the global financial game. Suddenly, world markets are improving despite dire warnings of further closings. It is/was the sheer greed of Banks and of market traders who gamble on share prices to make a quick buck that caused much of the trouble. Now, there are murmurs of better behaviour.

Alas Valhalla! After starting so well Europe fell away. Rose and Poulter were brilliant and un-beaten, but USA set the pace, finishing the day 5 1/2 to 2 1/2.

Saturday ◆ **SEPTEMBER 20**

Today, Europe's golfers have a chance to bounce back, just as global capitalism is attempting to do. A Times leader summed it up better than I could, so I'll quote: "It is as if the world's biggest banks have been on one giant bungee jump: their own customers, investors and employees have looked on powerless, as their individual financial futures plummeted and rebounded. The US Government has answered the bank panic of September 2008 with a promise to take all the dangerous debts out of the American banking system. It is, potentially, the biggest bail-out in the history of modern finance, and by ring fencing financial risk and therefore reducing fear in the credit markets it has restored confidence. The result was a £100 billion-plus rally on the London stock market yesterday, leaving the FTSE 100 index a mere two per cent lower than it had been at the beginning of the week."

The leader writer concludes, however, that the turmoil leaves literally hundreds of thousands of victims (ie those who worked for AIG, and Lehman Brothers) and for HBOS (quote) "They may yet have to live with the consequences of this week's firesale to Lloyds TSB." Many thousands may lose their jobs. These are the unintended consequences of a rescue that, hopefully, has saved world-wide disaster.

Sunday ◆ **SEPTEMBER 21**

It was not disaster at Valhalla today, just a sound beating. The USA won back the Ryder Cup 16 points to 11. I witnessed some of the finest golf ever seen, and it threw up new heroes, including

Boo Weakley and Ian Poulter who was Europe's star (he was my choice even before the contest began).

And then, the world. Don't ask me. The asylum outdid itself in murder and mayhem. * Bomb blast in Islamabad on Marriott Hotel killed 53 or more diners.* In China more than 53,000 children ill from contaminated baby milk. *More bomb blasts in Baghdad. * Kidnapping in Egypt.* Back home a father kills his two children then hangs himself after marriage breakdown. *Oil prices up with crude at $99 the barrel. * At the Labour Conference in Manchester Chancellor Darling gets a one minute standing ovation.

For me oh Lord, how much more dusting, sorting, washing up. I am just wasting away, a limping Martha, not even a Mary. And Jenny? The girl done good. Out with the giant box freezer, and in with our new, modest little number.

Monday ◆ SEPTEMBER 22

I need a prayer. Dear God, I feel the only way for the Western world, and the East, for that matter, to get better, to be more peaceful, less greedy and selfish, less violent, less criminal, less disturbed and unhappy, is to re-think the way we are, and re-order accordingly. This means stumbling back to the Christian ideal to doing what we know we should do, and not doing the things we ought not to do. Like prophets of old I would dearly like a sign, a conviction that you, the Almighty, are real, and that if we seek your spirit in all men we really can 'make the difference.

And PS: God. Can you make sure that Barack Obama becomes the next Pres of the USA. I believe he might bring a touch of sanity to our ailing asylum.

Tuesday ◆ SEPTEMBER 23

To students of the history of modern art the place to take some notes is the Scottish National Gallery. The current exhibition there is titled Impressionism and Scotland. So, today that is where we went. Some 320 works mostly on loan and all on view. Breathtaking. Two hours of blinding talent was all I could take, as in six rooms we moved from frame to frame to feast and to wonder, to salute and learn again what passion and genius is all about. All your favourites, and more, were there, from Degas's L'Absinthe to major impressionists including Manet, Monet, Sisley, Pissaro, Renoir, Whistler, Van Gogh, Cezanne, Gauguin, Toulouse-Lautrec and Matisse. The Glasgow Boys and Girls featured and so did the Scottish Colourists.

At Uni I studied Art History so I should have been prepared, but some of these glories, large and small, now came upon me like a flash of lightning. I limped away in an emotional turmoil and could not put the fire out until, with Chico and Jenny and Kathy I sat in the other La Petite Folie (in Randolph Place) with a bowl of steaming moules before me. And a glass of cooling white wine.

Wednesday ◆ SEPTEMBER 24

Over the silvery Tay to Dundee and the Rep to see Mother Courage by Brecht. Ach! Alas! All was grey, the setting, the costumes, the old wagon AND not least the utterly miserable story. I did not find it an inspiring saga of one woman's endless courage in the 30 Years War. It was all bullying. and bloodshed. I was not moved. I did not laugh or cry. But, again, the Company performed brilliantly. Anne Louise Ross as Mum gave 101 per cent. Her energy and stamina have to be seen to be believed.

Thursday ◆ SEPTEMBER 25

We made preparations for the lunch we are giving tomorrow for Betty and George Thomson. Betty and I both worked on The News Chronicle (Fleet Street) and George was The Scotsman's man in London. They married and have come to Lower Largo to visit George's family. We last met them at a re-union in London. We have planned a celebratory menu: fizz from New Zealand (better than much champagne) with canape (smoked salmon and olives stuffed with sun-dried tomato) For lunch, melon and Parma ham, followed by small bowls of chilled sweet potato and coconut soup; then fish pie with hot veg; then cheeses, of which

146

the one from North Sardinia and the organic Leicester were best. We finished the feast with fresh pineapple, and coffee.

Friday ◈ SEPTEMBER 26

It was marvellous to see my chums again. And not for a long time has this house burst with such laughter, shouts of joy as we recalled the good days. Fun, and by-lines galore. Over lunch Betty's story of how her forebears (17th century) bought land on which New York was built was hilarious. The family spent years trying to find the deeds of the sale, and longed for "the American money! " Alas, despite diligent, on the spot investigations, the deeds could not be found. Trips to the Big Apple were in vain. We sat at the table in the Bird Cage through the afternoon, then went up to the Golf House Club for a swift half before waving them farewell.

Saturday ◈ SEPTEMBER 27

After yesterday the asylum did not look so gloomy, but not all is fine and dandy. So far, the $700 billion planned to bale out Wall Street's ailing bankers has not materialised. Such uncertainty does nothing for confidence in high places. Here at home The Church of England's finances are under inspection as many of their investments could hardly be called ethical. It is all happening. PM Brown is in Washington. McCain and Obama are having a debate witnessed by 80 million viewers, and HM The Queen is to spend £7 million on a new private aircraft.

Happily, today, Life is still finding us out. Jenny has gone to the Ladies AGM (to be followed by another meeting with new committee members). Tonight she will be at the prize-giving dinner. She has won a coupla cups.

Sunday ◈ SEPTEMBER 28

Jenny decided to drive me to Meeting today. She took the dogs for a work-out on the West Sands. Later, as we watched Westwood losing the British Masters on the third play-off, Jean and

Alan Glen called in with a load of tomatoes from the farm "for Michael to make the soup."

Monday ◆ SEPTEMBER 29

We were astir at 6.a.m. as Jenny was being picked up at 7.40 by Anne Riddle and driven to Callander to play a round of golf with a bevy of former St. Leonards girls. I asked her to give my love to The Roman Camp Hotel, for it was there we spent the first few days of our honeymoon. I recall that the Manageress was called Miss Perfect, and that she had a well-trimmed black moustache. Truly! It was just a few days of a three-part honeymoon. The remainder of that holiday was spent on the Isle of Seal, and also dancing naked on the Braes of Balquider.

Today the news is a touch sunnier. The $700 billion being gifted to Wall Street is to be agreed by Congress and the Senate, and Washington swears that never again will the Administration bale out the fat cats there. "No more golden parachutes" Here, a further rescue has been provided by the British Government, now busy baling out Bradford and Bingley which crashed and which will be Nationalised, with Spain's Santander doing a little cherry-picking on the fringes.

So the Western World breathes a sigh of relief. We can all now get on with making the tomato soup. As I do so the pundits are still warning that the incipient recession, globally, has not yet bottomed out. (A large Belgian/European Bank is in trouble).

Tuesday ◆ SEPTEMBER 30

Ach! Not all is well. The Republicans in the House of Representatives have refused to ratify Bush's $700 billion bale- out for the fat cats of Wall Street. It is "a serious set-back." So, the nonsense continues as Banks generally sit tight, and refuse to lend as they lack confidence in the financial merry-go-round. If the stalemate continues we will have serious long-term trouble. So, the real story of A.D.2008 is all about sheer greed for big profits. The efforts to bring real aid to suffering communities here at home, or countries overseas pale into insignificance as any hope for a moral re-structure to society cracks and topples. It is little wonder that ordinary Joe and struggling Jill collapse on the sofa they could ill afford, switch on the telly and make their escape into sex, spectacle, the thrill of violence and, of course, the popular show called Strictly Come Dancing.

Wednesday ◆ OCTOBER 1

£55 TRILLION AWASH

Such a miserable Summer we have endured that when, as today, a bright, warm sun appears, we give the good Lord our thanks. The land and sea that were lost suddenly appear golden, and people like me in the asylum rejoice. It brings some cheer, as does the Autumn Journal of The Society of Authors. In it Andrew Taylor suggests a new game called Compose a Story in just Six Words. It was inspired by Ernest Hemingway. He gives a good example: 'For sale: baby shoes never worn.' Further delight follows with an example of 'inadvertent existential poetry' by courtesy of Donald Rumsfeld. He said: As we know.

> There are known knows.
> There are things we know we know,
> We also know
> There are known unknowns.

And it gets better. Hear this from George W. Bush: 'When I was coming up, it was a dangerous world, and you knew exactly who they were. It was us versus them, and it was clear who was them. Today we are not so sure who they are but we know they're there.' At a rally he was reported as saying :' I hope you leave here and walk out and say "What did he say? "(You bet we walked out!)

I have just invented some more Stories in Six Words. As follows: Doc said I had six weeks

- The lawyer's letter never reached her.
- She brained him - the 16th tee.
- He meant to give her Brandy.

Friday ◆ OCTOBER 2

Last night I witnessed the beginning of the end of life on Planet Earth. It reflected the dreams of Biblical prophets who told the story of the Earth covered by water, but I saw no Ark, and heard only the silent weeping of multitudes. It was the sad music of the orbs, of that band of throbbing light we call The Milky Way. And from across what was once flat land came a wavering invisibility, an unearthly haze alive with a dancing movement of light like electric discharges, and there was water everywhere with a myriad running streams. Two mortals appeared. I took them to a table in the kitchen, then to the empty dining room because there was a warm fire there in the grate. But, there was no saving of life as even the highest hills were disappearing beneath the water and the dancing, advancing, and impenetrable haze.

Friday ◆ OCTOBER 3

Today, the good, the saints, the ugly and the ancients gathered in the Golf House Club for a glass of wine as we remembered with love, affection, and sadness Barbara Grainger who died a week ago. Motor Neurone, that dread killer. Her husband Michael is a man I much admire. In the crowd he stood tall and looked weary, but his handshake was as firm as ever. He has daughters to help bind the wound.

Saturday ◆ OCTOBER 4

We rose at 6.00 a.m. Much to do. Packing the car, taking the dogs to the kennels for the day (and night), making breakfast and sandwiches, checking switches, washing, shaving, dressing, washing dishes, securing doors. Then we left to drive the 2 1/2 hours to Selkirk. The Band is to play for The Borders' Ball.

It was a terrible drive through heavy rain all the way and with roads in a mist of spray. Our first call was at The Garden House, the B&B where we would stay after the Ball. It turned out to be a modern building in a walled garden, the home of Robert and Hillary Dunlop. I rang the doorbell, but there was no answer, so I pushed the door open and walked in calling "Anyone there? Anyone home?" Answer came there none, so we carried our bags into one of the five bedrooms, and waited. It was mid-day when a car drove up and Mr. Dunlop appeared carrying bags and accompanied by two dogs. After eating our sandwiches and drinking our flask of soup we drove into Selkirk to the Victoria Hall and set up my kit on the stage. Then we returned to The Garden House and went to bed for a couple of hours' sleep. After changing into black tie order we met the rest of the Band who arrived at 4.00 p.m. and then drove to the hall as crowds of diners and dancers emerged from a fleet of cars and buses. We all drank fizz and ate canape in the lesser hall upstairs before being given our dinner in the dressing room behind the stage. By 9.45 p.m. we were on stage to play for 140 of the young and handsome until 2.30 a.m.

Sunday ◆ OCTOBER 5

Last night the Band was sober but played as if drunk and frankly the front line made a pigs ear of one of the reels. David, seated in front of me said he could not hear the drumming in spite of the fact that I was knocking the living daylights out of my kit I could hear very little at all except the roar from the floor. In fact, at the end, there was cheering and a standing ovation.

This morning, the Dunlop breakfast was bountiful. I had delicious scrambled eggs. Seated together in the small dining room we noisily discussed arrangements for the picnic Ball we hope to give which will signal our farewell, and thank you to our dancing friends as the Band closes down at the end of the year after 22 years.

Jenny and I then drove to Morebattle to take coffee with Joan and Ronald Wilson, and with son Robert who looks after the Hereford herd. It was great to see our farming friends again after a lapse of some four years. Then it was home to uplift Millie and Gemma from the kennels.

Monday ◈ OCTOBER 6

By 11.00 a.m. I had washed, shaved, made the breakfast, washed up, fed the dogs and driven to the village, bought the necessary then made the leek and potato soup ready for lunch. After which Jenny left to play bridge at Mae Noble's house. NEWS: Today the market fell 391 points. A recession seems inevitable.

Tuesday ◈ OCTOBER 7

Seek a Bright Angel. That is my tip for today. And once found, hang on tightly, because there are Dark Angels about as well. Consider this (I tell myself): An Almighty Being created the universe and all the other universes that scientists tell us exist. But a very busy Almighty cannot monitor every single galaxy out there. He has apportioned bands of Bright Angels to serve with and for him. But Bright cannot exist without Dark to show that Bright is a reality. So, brooding Dark Angels are always on hand with a million mischiefs to deploy. They are leavening the current recession, the sheer greed, the lack of confidence, and the obscene behaviour of the Fat Cats. In reality the financial market is in a mess because WE are in a mess. We need an open-minded, and a fair minded approach, with honest dealing. We need to re-discover a moral fortitude that works, and to do this we have to sustain the Bright Angels to assist us. It is an open choice. Love a Dark Angel and die. Chose a Bright Angel and live. Take a return ticket to the collective unconscious. Bright Angels cannot shine without humans that are whole.

Wednesday ◈ OCTOBER 8

The great and the good in the financial world – or what is left of them – worked all last night to bring a solution to the banking crisis and the predicted economic downturn. By 5.00 a.m. today they had it. Our banks will be part-nationalised and, with a gift of £50 billion, saved from disaster. No-one knows whether this tactic will succeed. As wiseacres are saying "We do not know how it will work out because we have never been here before

We are in un-charted waters." Everyone hopes their savings will now be secured, but it seems that pensions will take a hit. This bumpy ride for the economy will, we are told, last well into 2009. A half per cent. cut in the interest rate has been scheduled here, in the US and in other European countries.

Thursday ◆ OCTOBER 9

The news is dire. Banks and charities here invested in Banks in Iceland, and they have not just 'frozen' they seem to have sunk without trace, and now British investors are shouting for their money back. None the less, we were cheery here, as Mark and Verity called in for lunch with their two kids, Charlotte (nearly three) and Jamie (seven months). We enjoyed Jenny's Matelot's Tart – but it wasn't easy eating it as children come first at the table or on the floor. In the evening Jenny went to our local History Society meeting to hear a talk by Dr. Geoffrey Millar M.B., Ch., B., FRCSEd., FRCOphth.

Friday ◆ OCTOBER 10

The moaning and the groaning from financial gurus is terrible. World markets have toppled. Global recession to get worse. Oddly the war in Afghanistan is being won by the Taliban using thousands of mobile phones through which to shout their political publicity. Here, debts and financial disaster are being measured in trillians of dollars. And guess what – it is announced that Doctor Death is in town with advice and techniques on how to commit suicide when you get too old or too depressed to live in the asylum any longer.

Saturday ◆ OCTOBER 11

Carolyn and Keith McDonald said come and have a drink at seven, then we'll go and have supper at Anstruther Golf Club – "We have booked a table. Cheap and cheerful, but the food is said to be rather good."

It was. The room is small and plain, but, true, the food was excellent, imaginative, not expensive, and the service was prompt and cheery.

Sunday ◆ OCTOBER 12

Jenny to her church. My back told me to rest. So I did. The IMF boss is reported as saying the world is on the brink of "financial meltdown." Share prices last week took a dive by at least 20 per cent., and might drop by another 20 per cent. before stabilising. The Stock Market is said to be in a state of panic. The G7 countries have not yet worked out a rescue plan and, sadly, some 1,000 Scots a month are declaring themselves bankrupt.

Monday ◆ OCTOBER 13

Jenny's Bridge Four came to the cottage and shrieked their way through three hours of double dealing in the sitting room, so I started editing some pages of this Journal. The sun was blinding in a huge sky, and I had hoped to play a few holes on the links. However, one of the tyres on the buggy was flat. The wheel had been fitted the wrong way round, and we could not change it. Happily a genius of a groundsman with strength and skill could. And did.

Astonishing news! We have been asked to have supper with Valerie, the very Valerie of previous cancelled invitations. We wait with fingers crossed, but it is TRUE! At seven we drove to her cottage and there she was, tall, statuesque in black and with a brilliant cloud of silver hair. With her was Fay, the chubby sister of David Steele's wife, and Rose with husband Callum. It was the Far East that had come to Valerie's rescue. Two persons arrived bearing cardboard boxes which contained our supper. A Chinese carry-oot!

Tuesday ◆ OCTOBER 14

A Banker declared "There is an animal loose in the world of finance". So, what is the animal called? Inflation. Highest for 14 years. Mass unemployment likely. In Britain, the US and Europe there is £55 trillion awash. And Banks generally still will not communicate with each other. The vital money - go- round is stuck.

Wednesday ◈ OCTOBER 15

The IMF boss repeats: " the world is on the brink of financial meltdown" Share prices dived by 20 per cent. Stock markets "in a state of panic" The shadow of unemployment looms yet larger. Nevertheless, here we had good cheer. This morning, along with hundreds of over-fifties, we assembled in the Church's community hall for the annual flu jab. I expect we'll get flu all the same!

Thursday ◈ OCTOBER 16

We drove over to St, Margaret's Hospital in Dunfermline for Jenny to have a scan on her neck. The entrance hall is like a shopping mall café. It is monstrous, with a multitude of people old and young seated at tables drinking coffee and munching food. The place seems to be in uproar with kids hurtling around. After climbing stairs and trudging along endless corridors we found the scanning room. Peace at last. The scan took 15 minutes and I watched the screen to see Jenny's blood flowing along nicely in full technicolour. Looked okay to me, and the scanning chap seemed to think Jenny will live.

Friday ◈ OCTOBER 17

She was up and about early to play a medal round. Thankfully the rain cleared away. She was home by 4.00 p.m. I spent several hours editing earlier chapters of this Journal. Tomorrow we play a birthday gig at Carberry Tower near Inveresk.

Saturday ◈ OCTOBER 18

We left at teatime (black tie order) to be at Carberry by 6.15 p.m. It is a handsome castle more than 450 years old and I have a suspicion that Mary Queen of Scots might have had a bit of how's yer father there with Bothwell. And why not? She had a pretty rotten life in Scotland. Maybe her ghost will be present to dance with her amour to our music. We needed someone to play to because of the 120 birthday guests 90 per cent were aged over 80, and not inclined to jump about.

A strong sense of history. The original 'Tower' was known to Monks in the 11th century. This century it was the home of the Elphinstone family – Lady E was the sister of the late Queen Mother. The place was passed to The Church of Scotland to become a youth and conference centre, then ownership was transferred to the Carberry Trust until four years ago when it became a charity (Gartmore House). It is a warren of drawing rooms and has bedrooms as it is now used as a posh B&B.

Before playing we had to stand with the guests for ages drinking champagne cocktails until we were seated for a splendid refection. Sitting opposite me was a blonde bombshell from Sweden with national decolletage, and to my left was a male Roman Catholic giant, so we had an argument about God and worship. As for the music (after birthday speeches) we played in a carpeted room but hardly any guests danced. We tempted them with the Charleston and Black Bottom. Several more took to the floor when, as a final hurrah, we played an Eightsome and a Strip the Willow. Jenny had left to have her supper with Chico and Kathy but, she found her way back at midnight to uplift me and drive back home. Bed by 2.30 a.m.

Sunday ◆ OCTOBER 19

Pretty drowsy today. All that standing about with cocktails last evening has left me kinda injured, so I snored in front of TV rugby, while Jenny sensibly went to bed.

Monday ◆ OCTOBER 20

It's her birthday. The sky cleared and the sun was dazzling. I wanted to take her out to dinner tonight, but she refused, saying she would rather eat at home. A clever ruse. It has to be Thai Chicken and that means I will be the chef. I have remembered to give her a card, a necklace and earrings, and some smoked salmon and asparagus as they are something we can share (a cunning trick!). She really deserves so much more. After all, she is a saint, a positive pearl of a girl. After lunch she left to play Bridge. Before leaving she handed me an e-mail. Sadness. It was from Fr. Botulus to say that yesterday Fr. Banquo had died after a fall at home. He was Brig. Frank Coutts, a splendid Monk of St Giles. Jenny and I – and everyone – admired and loved him.

Tuesday ◆ **OCTOBER 21**

Yesterday The Ministry of Defence announced that in 1991 an Al Italia flight heading for Heathrow had a narrow miss with an Unidentified Object (UF0).The event was on the secrets list and was not disclosed until now. This news was unusual as such encounters and sightings were never publicly confirmed. Pilots and others who swear that they "saw something" were instructed to say nothing no matter how positive the sighting had been.

This was all very well until (yesterday) a Mr. Milton Torres, now living in Miami, spoke up. In the Second World War he was a fighter pilot based in East Anglia. He took off from the airfield under instructions to locate and destroy an unidentified object which had appeared on radar screens. Find it and shoot it down, he was told. At 32,000 ft over Norwich he spotted it and locked on ready to destroy.

He said "It was about the size of an aircraft carrier and was moving very fast" To get within firing range he switched to his afterburn and gave chase. "But it was impossible" he said. "As I approached the thing moved faster than the speed of light. It just disappeared."

Back at base he reported what he had found and was told to say nothing to anyone. If he did not keep his trap shut he would be dismissed the service. So, the gallant Pilot Torres said not one word –- until yesterday. The encounter, he said, had terrified him. His account lends credence to the many reports of findings of this kind, and his report was in fact confirmed by fellow pilots who had noted similar phenomena. We should not be surprised. Our galaxy comprises many millions of stars and inevitably very many planets that could support some form of life. All those "flying saucers" that people have reported must be small reconnaissance vehicles despatched by their Mother – the aircraft carrier – to take a closer look at us. I wish I could e-mail God, for I am sure He would confirm this.

Coming down to Earth, Jenny has just disappeared, almost at the speed of light, to make up a golfing four with friends of the Hardies. Afterwards we are bidden to take supper with them and the Hardies tonight.

Wednesday ◈ OCTOBER 22

We were eight to the table last night, the other guests being Brian and Connie Simmers, and Alastair and Heather Burnet. All strong golfers and close friends, so conversation roared along and for five hours there was roof-raising laughter and good cheer with food and wine keeping energy levels on a high.

Doom and gloom were just around the corner of course. Today the Big R was writ large across the UK. Recession confirmed by King at the Bank of England and by Prime Minister Brown. The retail trade, with stores like Homebase and B&Q is reporting more losses, and global markets across the world are on a continuing downturn. We were not cheered to learn that shadow Chancellor Osborne (£4 million) might have been discussing funds for the Conservative Party with the Russian billionaire Oleg Deripaska (£16 billion) who moored his massive yacht off Corfu. Nat Rothschild (hedge-fund) was present in his island villa. Any charges about funding the Conservative Party have been denied. But who knows what really goes on when the wealthy big hitters get together over holiday drinks. If there was a fly on the bulkhead, or on the villa walls it surely had a diamond and emerald body with wings of gold and platinum legs.

Today, there are more millions on the move with a lift-off and a woosh in India as a rocket, with satellite, was launched on a recce to the moon. I bet many of the poverty stricken millions in their steaming shanties would have liked a share of those dollars and rupees that the mission is devouring. For so many people in the asylum life must be somewhere between an unavoidable disaster and a joke. Or, more importantly, a cry for help.

Thursday ◆ OCTOBER 23

The outlook for Britain's small businesses is questionable. They require help from the Banks to be able to continue. But many a Bank holds back because they believe the businesses that want a life-saving loan may not be a good bet simply because, unless they can trade profitably they will be unable to repay the interest on the loan. It's a catch-22 situation, but The Money-go-Round must be restored if small businesses are to be saved. However, there are lots of people who will not be touched by the credit crunch. MPs and politicians generally will be okay, and so will GPs and Lawyers. First Div. and Premier Div. footballers will not feel the draft as many of them earn £80,000 (or more) per week. I have always felt that Ladies's hairdressers and manufacturers of womens' knickers will remain in healthy credit come what may! And how about Senator McCain's running mate Sarah Palin. She spent $90,000 on fashionable outfits to look sassy at the Republican convention.

Friday ◆ OCTOBER 24

The UK economy continues to shrink, 0.5 per cent in four months. According to the boffins we are entering a once in a lifetime crisis, "the largest of its kind in human history" Dealers on falling world markets have their heads in their hands. So, is anyone winning? Yes, the food take-away trade is doing well. It is a cheaper meal at home than in the restaurant. Also home movies (ie: DVDs) are doing better trade (why go to the cinema). Cobblers are doing better than ever before. People are not buying new shoes they are repairing their old baffies. And chimney sweeps are doing better business as people open up their chimneys to kindle coal fires and keep warm!

Saturday ◆ OCTOBER 25

Mark Wang called in this morning with his two young daughters, Inga and Lisabet. So we had coffee and a rolly-poly time with the dogs. Mark's landscape business continues to thrive, with 25 employees. The company has large and smaller contracts throughout England and Scotland. He works hard, but makes time to relax. On Boxing Day, with wife Jayne and the family (4) he is flying to Panama to board a cruise ship and do the Caribbean islands for a fortnight. His brother Magnus is also a success, and is in charge of BMW in Edinburgh. I suspect the brothers have profited from the genes they inherited from their parents Mary and Peter.

Sunday ◈ OCTOBER 26

The church here has a lively congregation, and there was a spirit of goodness and the usual anticipation as old, young and very young rustled into their pews. Instead of going to Meeting I accompanied Jenny who was to read the second Lesson after Dr. Gilly Thompson who read the first. They were both loud and clear. The Anderson family were also present as Peter and Margaret's babe, Harry Stephen Bell, was to be baptised. All was well, and all was very well.

Monday ◈ OCTOBER 27

Today a page in Army history (Scotland) was turned as a vast number of men and women attended the funeral of Brigadier Frank Coutts CBE who died seven days ago aged 90. Jenny and I attended the Service of Thanksgiving in Canongate Kirk which is spacious but was not large enough to accommodate all those who wished to say farewell to a wonderful guy. There was a half page Obituary in The Scotsman. It described his Army career, his rugby (he was an internationalist and President of the SRU) and his writing (two books). We knew Frank as Father Banquo, which was his name in The Monks of St. Giles, and like everyone else we found him a delightful man with a great sense of humour. He was an Elder of the Church, a strong yet very kind man with outstanding qualities of leadership. He will be sorely missed.

Tuesday ◈ OCTOBER 28

The news on the financial front continues to dismay and like many others (I am sure) I am beginning to get further confused by the talk of dollars and pounds in trillions. No cheer in the asylum. Not one small glimmer of comfort.

Wednesday ◈ OCTOBER 29

No. It is cold comfort. No good news. *In the Democratic Republic of The Congo, a nation larger than Europe, rebel forces attack the Government as thousands flee for safety with no food or shelter *Earthquake in Pakistan with many fatalities *Hungarian economy failing and being bailed out by the IMF * Hedge Funds losing billions after mad speculation on Volkswagon shares *BP sitting on incredible profits, but even with the price of crude falling they refuse to lower prices at the pumps. A small hurrah. This evening we go to Edinburgh. A private view of paintings for sale with proceeds to Macmillan Cancer Support. Chico Ramos is exhibiting.

Thursday ◈ OCTOBER 30

The exhibition, called 'The Art of Life,' was sponsored by Scottish Widows and held in the Lyon and Turnbull auction hall. There were some 300 paintings priced from £60 to £3,500. Macmillan receive 100 per cent (and in some cases 50 per cent) of the price of the paintings sold. Chico showed three. I liked two of them. Many of the items on view were ghastly, but this was not the point, the cancer fund will profit. Afterwards we drove over to Chico and Kathy's home for a hearty guinea fowl casserole and big slurps of wine. I took them two bottles from the professor, and some nuts I had roasted. Kathy's lady cousin from Twickenham was at the table, as was Tony (Chico's Portuguese friend) and his wife. A delight to meet all three.

To bed at 1.00 a.m. listening to news. Furore! The BBC had allowed two jokers (Brand and Ross) to air some mild filth. Many thousands of viewers/listeners protested, so now the Beeb is taking the flak. The editor of the programme should walk before standards fall still further.

Friday ◆ OCTOBER 31

The Democratic Republic of Congo has long been warring with itself and now the situation is even worse. Rebel forces are advancing on the Eastern border town of Goma and driving 300,000 families from their homes. The UN Peace Keeping Force appears unable to cope with the rebels, and aid agencies are struggling to get food to the starving refugees. Politicians are calling it a humanitarian disaster. The rebels are savages, raping and killing at will.

Here at home Brand and Ross are in trouble. Brand says he will never work again for the BBC, and has taken off for America. Ross has been suspended with the loss of a minimal part of his £6 million salary. He just smiled and threw a massive Halloween party.

Saturday ◆ NOVEMBER 1

MAYHEM IN MUMBAI

Crazy. Not a breath of wind stirs and the sun shouts from a clear sky. It's Summer. In the Bird Cage the temperature rose to 80 degrees F by 11.00 a.m. Time for gardening and shirt sleeves.

Sunday ◆ NOVEMBER 2

Another brilliant, sunny Summer day. At Meeting I picked up the little red book called Advices and Queries. Try as I may I cannot get away from the good sense and spiritual guidance the Quakers live by. (Quote): Para 22. 'Respect the wide diversity among us in our lives and relationships. Refrain from making prejudiced judgements about the life journeys of others. Do you foster the spirit of mutual understanding and forgiveness which our discipleship asks of us? Remember that each one of us is unique, precious, a child of God.'

The basis of these advices stems from a Friends Yearly Meeting in 1682. The total of today's 42 advices was 'grown' from an original three questions which early Friends posed as a form of discipline.

Monday ◈ NOVEMBER 3

Young Lewis Hamilton has been declared winner of the Formula One championship. He won by a whisker. There are great celebrations to come as his undoubted skill is applauded. I have never understood what this championship achieves, but feel sure it is a dreadful waste. We are repeatedly told that even driving saloon cars is having a seriously bad effect on global warming, so what is the world-wide racing car business doing to it. Sounds mad to me.

The Monks' Chapter in Edinburgh tonight produced a full house and several brilliant verses. The standard is rising month by month and tonight there were at least three excellent songs at the piano. I withheld my offering for next month.

Tuesday ◈ NOVEMBER 4

Starvation and fighting in Somalia. The media will barely cover the facts because, of course, today 130 million people in America go to the polls to elect a new President who, it is said, will be the most powerful man in the world. So far the polls favour Obama, but the result is not written in stone – yet. Whoever wins may not be the most powerful man. Like it or no there is a tide of power from China and also from the Gulf states. They could hold the world to ransom (oil) as could Russia. One thing is sure: the new man will inherit a failing economic situation at home and a confused and very stormy financial climate world-wide.

Wednesday ◈ NOVEMBER 5

America has a new voice. A bold and hopeful voice. For the first time in history the President will be a black man and the United States of America will be united as never before. Barack Obama, President Elect, is setting out to prove that his vast nation can pull together. A record number of voters across the continent – including the first time young voters – is making it perfectly clear that this change is what they desire. The White

House, led by a new team, will give America, and Europe too, the hope and the confidence it so badly needs. Constraints and difficulties will no doubt be legion. There will be set-backs and disappointments. But now millions are beginning to sense a new world is dawning. Historians will not find it difficult to devine how Obama's spectacular win came about. First, to win elections you require enormous sums of money. Obama raised a vast amount. Second, you need highly professional planning and organisation. Obama's team had it. Third you need a leader who can inspire. During the long, exhausting election, Obama summoned the energy, the imagination, and the presence to which the electorate of all colours and creeds clearly responded. Early this morning (2.00 a.m.) I went to bed happy, knowing that, long before the majority of States had declared, the right man had triumphed and, as Americans might say, a whole new ball game had begun.

Thursday ◆ **NOVEMBER 6**

Three inch thick plate glass screens shield Obama when he addresses the multitude. They are bullet-proof. There will also be tight security for his family. The worst scenario would be the kidnapping of his two young daughters. We do not want to look on the dark side, but the fact is Presidents have been targets and probably always will be. In December 1862 President Abraham Lincoln gave his annual message to Congress sans protection, despite dangerous times. He said 'Fellow citizens, we cannot escape history. We of this Congress and this administration, will be remembered in spite of ourselves. No personal significance, or insignificance, can spare one or other of us. The fiery trial through which we pass, will light us down, in honor or dishonor, to the latest generation. We say we are for the Union. The world will not forget that we say this. We know how to save the Union. The world knows we do know how to save it. We – even we here – hold the power and bear the responsibility. In giving freedom to the slave, we assure freedom to the free – honorable alike in what we give, and what we preserve. We shall nobly save, or meanly lose, the last best hope of earth. Other means may succeed; this could not fail. The way is plain, peaceful, generous, just – a way which if followed, the world will forever applaud, and God must forever bless."

Three years after delivering this address Lincoln was assassinated. He was a Republican. In our own time we remember only too well what befell the Democratic President Jack Kennedy. Today, with fingers crossed, the asylum somehow survives and we pray that Obama will see us, as well as America, safely through his global watch.

Friday ◈ NOVEMBER 7

The asylum is falling headlong into the history books. Today Obama will give his first news conference after winning the election, and he will have to pull back on some of the promises he made before the true scale of the global economic downturn was fully appreciated.

Here at home –– surprise, surprise. Against all predictions the Glenrothes by-election has been won by Labour (majority 7,000). A defeat for the Scottish Nationalists which brings a smile to the face of Gordon Brown.

More good news: * Banks beginning to pass on to customers easier movement on mortgages following the cut in the interest rate by a massive 1.5%. * British troops to be out of Iraq by April next year. * £300 million worth of drugs confiscated from a yacht apprehended off the Irish coast.

The bad news: *The violence in East Congo and Rwanda increases as the tribes clash. * Here in Fife Jenny's sister was rushed to hospital yesterday. An emergency. We suspect a heart attack. Touch and go. * The credit crunch is biting. In the USA 240,000 jobs were lost during October.

Personal: As a former journalist I am filled with admiration for a news reporter called Emma Hurd. She covers ghastly and dangerous situations world-wide and remains as cool and collected as if she was attending a sunny BBQ in a Surrey back garden. Currently she is in the thick of it in East Congo. Take care Emma, you're a darlin' and we need you!

Saturday ◆ **NOVEMBER 8**

The Band is planning details of our final gig in January next year, and I thought I would draft a Press release. I have written:

(Headline): 500 Year Old Band aids Motor Neurone Research

The Auld Reekie Scottish Dance Band is holding a dance at George Watson's College, Edinburgh for 300 of their supporters on Saturday January 17th 2009. All monies donated will go to The Euan MacDonald Centre for Motor Neurone Disease Research. The occasion will also mark the ending of the Band's playing life of a quarter of a century. The combined ages of the seven 'regulars' is 500. Originally formed by Edinburgh lawyer William Leslie, the Band has performed at venues ranging throughout the UK from the far North down to Kent, and from Yorkshire and Cheshire and most Scottish counties to Ireland and Austria. Band leader Rachel Fraser (accordion) says: "We are amateurs of course, and we've enjoyed almost every minute of every gig. But we feel now is the time sadly to say farewell. Saturday will be our final fling, and as well as the traditional reels and jigs we'll be playing Twenties standards and jazz. Saturday's support for the MacDonald Centre is our serious aim." (NOTE: added to this Journal, after the event. In fact 650 people wanted to say farewell to the Band, so we had to hold two farewell dances on consecutive evenings. People were generous. We raised some £31,000 for research into Motor Neurone disease, and were astonished and delighted).

Today the Band is playing in Edinburgh at a party for the choir of St, Giles Cathedral.

News: A school has collapsed in Haiti killing many children, and there is a hurricane trying to destroy Jamaica. Jenny's sister is recovering in hospital. Her dog sleeps on our bed.

Sunday ◆ **NOVEMBER 9**

It was an odd gig last night. In Edinburgh's Walpole Hall we played reels for the young supporters of the Choir which is raising money for a tour. It was like a village hop and ended at midnight.

We were tired today and I felt rather fed up as I had handed the Band a draft of a possible Press Release for our farewell charity dance. I asked for their comments and received only one response. It came from Peter who declared "We are not amateurs!"

All right. Neither are we professionals, so what the hell are we? If we can agree a Press Release we should add that those who cannot attend our farewell dance might like to send a donation to motor neurone research

Monday ◈ NOVEMBER 10

I took a cracked molar to the dental surgeon in St. Andrews and he made a repair which I trust will last (£45). Then from Mellis I purchased Parma ham and some cheese for tomorrow night's supper.

TV showed us Prime Minister Brown addressing a subdued crowd at the Lord Mayor of London's Banquet. He spoke confidently of "an unprecedented period of global change." Our aim would be to forge "a new multilateralism," and he hoped the US - Europe alliance would provide leadership in the new world. He felt the election of Obama was a source of hope and inspiration, and he called for greater tolerance and understanding, plus a reduction of Arms.

There will be many more similar messages come January when Obama moves into The White House. I believe he is our best hope as he struggles with world-wide financial chaos and war. Today was red poppy day when we salute and remember all who lost their lives in two world wars.

Tuesday ◈ NOVEMBER 11

It is Armistice Day. The two wars to end all war produced incredible bravery and sacrifice, but they did not end war. We have had years of violence since then, and currently we are grieving for those killed in three on-going wars – Iraq, Afghanistan, and The Middle East where Israel and the Palestinians are still shooting or bombing each other. The Congo has endured violence and mayhem for fifty years and the slaughter still continues. The shards of hope and prayer lie at our feet. Humankind may long for peace, So why, in a so-called enlightened 21st century do we not do it.

Looking through my 2002 journal I found a Muslim comment on prayer. (quote):"Prayer should not be merely a series of words and movements practised occasionally without thought, it must be established in the heart if it is to give the desired result. Prayer should be established in the home, in the family, and finally in the community as a whole."

Wednesday ◆ NOVEMBER 12

There have been more killings in Afghanistan, Iraq and, it seems, in Pakistan. In a newly published survey two thirds of those questioned said they wanted our troops to be brought home now. It was no surprise that most women supported an immediate withdrawal. The Government, and 24 per cent of those polled, said they wanted the British fighting force to remain. After seeing a snatch of PM's Questions in the Commons yesterday the Party games, the anger and rows gave little hope that anything will change, and lives will continue to be lost.

After a visit to Suzie for physiotherapy the verdict on my right painful ankle is that I have damaged the tendons there. The foot has to have ice bags placed on it, and I am told not to walk or play gigs. Difficult. This evening Peter and Mary Wang and Richard and Paddy Harden are coming for supper in the Birdcage which involves much to-ing and fro-ing. We are offering pate as canape, Melon and Parma Ham, followed by a small 'interval' dish of Sweet Potato and Coconut broth. The main course will be Jenny's Boeuf Bourguignonne with fresh veg, then Apple Pie with ice cream and coffee. (Sparkling wine, with Minervois from the professor).

Thursday ◆ NOVEMBER 13

To St. Andrews again. Jenny to dentist. I bought two 12 inch sticks of Spanish chourizo the other day. Today they disappeared. I had left them on the worktop in the kitchen, forgetting that

Gemma is a high jump champion. The wrapping on the floor indicated that the contents had to be consumed today – so presumably Gemma can read as well as leap. I guess she and Millie enjoyed every mouthful.

Friday ◈ NOVEMBER 14

The dogs to the kennels and ourselves to Yorkshire for tomorrow night's gig, the annual ball that raises money for Riding for The Disabled. Road works and accidents (as usual) delayed our arrival at Four Gables in Boston Spa. It is a beautifully preserved Arts and Crafts house (1900) up a lane off the main drag. A quiet and comfortable B&B. For me Boston Spa offers two other joys: beautiful Georgian town houses, and an excellent Thai restaurant. Tonight it was crowded, but I had booked a table. We enjoyed our supper, except I succeeded in throwing a glass of water into Jenny's lap. She had to sit for two hours in wet knickers. Most wives would have (a) slapped my face, (b) stalked out, or (c) started divorce proceedings. But not Jenny. She laughed. She shone. She was happy. But then, what else would you expect when you are married to a saint.

Saturday ◈ NOVEMBER 15

The little duties life demands. A visit to the retail outlet to purchase a Christmas present for Michael Dickson – a cashmere scarf. Then to brother Owen in Fulford. He is ancient, and frail, but had good colour. A survivor despite Parkinsons and dementia. Nancy copes very well. Then back to Four Gables for a pre-gig rest. At 7.30 p.m. we found the hall –- we had been there before for supper and dancing. It is an early Georgian monument, its faded, echoing rooms rarely used, but still a home to our host and hostess. Tonight they had invited a pre-dance party of thirty friends and family to supper. And kindly included us. We discovered we had stepped back in time to an era of courtly manners, and extremely polite conversation. We joined together over drinks before a large blazing hearth. Eccentric canape were handed round with champagne (eg: boiled potatoes cut in half and dabbed with crème fraiche, and toast buttered with hummus) and I was addressed by a very tall, hyphenated person who spoke softly without moving his lips (Eton or Harrow I suspected). At his side was a dark-haired small man given to astonishing cheerfulness and who shouted through shining teeth. He was 100 per cent. Bertie Wooster. "I say! " he cried. "How simply spiffing! A 1! Golly, did she REALLY! That's going it a bit, what !" Pure 1920's. And we loved it. A candlelight dinner was served with 17 guests at a vast mahogany table bearing solid, shining silver candelabra and, rather oddly, plain kitchen cutlery. I was seated at a table for six. I could not deal with the venison or the carrots for fear of breaking my teeth, but the blood red wine was – you might say – exceeding good, and the elegant ladies to my right and left were enchanting. Such charm and old world courtesy I have not experienced for years. They spoke and ate with great delicacy.

The dancing followed in Tadcaster's Riley Smith Hall where, on the big stage, festooned with balloons, we have played each November for the past 15 years for about 150 of this charity-minded county set. This was our last appearance for them, and at 2.00 a.m. after the National Anthem we were given a stamping and shouting standing ovation. Farewell gifts were brought up to the stage, a box of champagne, also individual bottles of The Famous Grouse, and for Band leader Rachel a bouquet fit for a Prima Ballerina! There were profuse thank you's and sad goodbyes. We had played famously and there was regret. They will not see our like again, and I for one will miss what has always been an enjoyable and worthwhile gig in the county where I was born.

Sunday ◆ NOVEMBER 16

A sleepy, familiar breakfast at Four Gables. Then we packed and drove the A1 M to Edinburgh, then Fife and home to collect the dogs from the kennels and fall asleep before we could get to bed. The house was freezing. Boiler trouble. We trust the central heating will be repaired tomorrow.

Monday ◆ NOVEMBER 17

Enter the gas man. He is fat, conversational, and clearly knows his stuff. After lengthy exploration of the CH system he decided a major overhaul will be necessary, involving new parts. He hopes to return on Wednesday, or Thursday with all the bits and pieces to get the system working again. Meantime we are using the three electric fires we luckily possess.

Tuesday ◆ NOVEMBER 18

She is beautiful and currently lying off the Somalia coast. The super tanker called Sirius Star has been hi-jacked by pirates and contains 100 million dollars worth of oil, and two Brits are among the crew. A massive ransom will be demanded. The money the pirates will receive from the owners of the tanker will, it is supposed, go to terrorist groups,

More news: Australia is suffering from a massive plague of locusts. The swarms are up to three miles long! In the UK it is bees. They are not swarming, they are fast disappearing with – say the pundits – serious consequences for our crops.

Wednesday ◆ NOVEMBER 19

The gas man called again today. He suspects that, after all, the CH system is working correctly. We think, and hope, that it is. So does he. It will avoid pulling the entire system to pieces and re-assembling which would take hours to complete.

Thursday ◆ NOVEMBER 20

Aid agencies are appealing for money to assist the refugees in East Congo, but an expert says money will not help. "There is plenty of money sloshing around," he says. "What is required is an effort by the UN and other nations to solve the overall prob-lem – tribal strife and slaughter – which afflicts this vast country," It seems that 'the war' which has been waged now for some 50 years probably concerns the vast reserves of mineral wealth.

In the Western World it is also sheer greed that is halting the solution to the global downturn. The Banks in the US which have accepted massive assistance from the Fed are simply refusing to co-operate one with another, and to lend to customers. Thus, the vital money-go-round is jammed. It will, it is said, cause even further disasters. There's more trouble, too. The current US Government is refusing to bale out the giant motor industry (GM and the others) who are begging for funds.

Friday ◆ NOVEMBER 21

Hooray ! Some 300 invitations to the Band's farewell have now gone out. "The Auld Reekie Scottish Dance Band" reads the heading. "Final Farewell Picnic Supper Dance in The Main Hall, George Watson's College, Colinton Road, Edinburgh. By kind permission of the Governors. On Saturday 17 January 2009 in aid of The Euan MacDonald Centre for Motor Neurone Disease Research. Dress: Black tie. Arrival and supper from 7.30 p.m. Dancing 9.30 p.m. Carriages 12.30 p.m.

The Auld Reekie Scottish Dance Band: Rachel Fraser, accordion, Ian MacMillan, accordion, David Todd, fiddle, Iain King, fiddle, Donald MacDonald, fiddle, Peter Gordon, piano, Michael Gilderdale, drums." An accompanying letter hopes respondents might care to give a donation to the Centre "at a suggested level of £25 a head."

Other news: Chancellor angry. UK Banks not lending to small businesses. UK car industry also in trouble, with Honda stopping production for two months. And now 123 houses per day are being re-possessed. Unemployment is rising and will increase.

Saturday ◆ NOVEMBER 22

Jenny's sister is still in hospital so we went to visit her, ten floors up in a tower block. She seemed, as people say, to be on the mend but still cannot walk more than a few steps. In the small ward for four beds she sat in a chair and talked non stop for two hours. To hear what she had to say was not always easy. A mother with four children was visiting another bed. The kids roared around shouting their heads off and demanding toys. They appeared to be uncontrollable.

Sunday ◈ **NOVEMBER 23**

David Peebles is looking in for supper tonight, so we spent time in the kitchen preparing a meal. Jenny made a pheasant casserole, and an apple crumble while I prepared veg, and melon with Parma Ham, also a sardine pate in croustades. For future use I also made a spicy parsnip soup and laid the table and set up the wine. Small duties, but we still enjoy entertaining (until we have to clear up afterwards.)

This morning we awoke to snow. A white world. I decided to risk a drive to Meeting. The roads were reasonably dangerous. However, I made St. Andrews only to be met at the Meeting House door by a young woman saying that the place was closed and the Meeting was being held in Trinity Church Hall the better to accommodate Friends from Edinburgh. The streets had not been cleared, which made walking perilous, so I simply turned around and drove back home. I vented my frustration in the kitchen by slicing onions and carrots.

We enjoyed David's company at table and there was much talk about the local Church of Scotland affairs and general worry about the moguls who manipulate matters at the HQ in George Street.

Monday ◈ **NOVEMBER 24**

I have started writing Christmas Cards, wanting the tedious business out of the way. We usually send about 170 each year, but I am determined we should cut numbers back. Today is supposed to be the big pre-Budget Day with Chancellor Darling telling the nation how the Government plans to get us out of the recession. For months we have had so much ranting and raving about the global turndown we are all going to be yawning.

Tuesday ◆ NOVEMBER 25

The Chancellor, with a snowball for a head, yesterday told the Commons what it expected to hear. Economic growth for this year – 0.75 %. Borrowing, currently at £76 billion, will rise to £118 billion next year. Salaries at over £125,000 p.a. will be taxed at 45%. VAT at 171/2% reduced to 15% for one year only. There will be a child poverty Bill, and more for Pensioners and Job Centres. Small businesses will be allowed to pay their taxes over extended periods (ie: when they wish). For motorists fuel efficiency bands will be phased in, there will be more 'mortgage rescue' and social housing will be modernised. The duty on alcohol, tobacco and petrol will be raised. "The unprecedented global crisis called for unprecedented measures," said the snowball. The Opposition shouted rubbish, it was all a dangerous and wicked gamble. It appeared that a Tory Government would do little more than sit on its hands and wait for the crisis to pass.

A lone voice supported the Chancellor's measures. Caan (one of the Dragons from Dragons Den) liked the big borrow, saying the confident, optimistic strategy was needed. Of course it was a gigantic gamble. If it worked the Government would have confounded all critics. If it failed it would be goodbye Labour.

So. We are gobsmacked. And utterly depressed by all the gobbledegook that is pouring in torrents from politicians and commentators alike. We are reaching screaming point in the asylum, we are a house totally out of order because we know there are no certainties. No-one can tell what the national and global situation will be like two years or ten years from now. But then, what's new? We are a nation of gamblers, the world is a big gamble. Bankers, corporations and governments live by gambling. The roll of the dice may not be nice, but it's the only throw the punters know. So – we are all to blame. A giant called GREED strides the globe, from Japan, China and India to Europe, the USA. And little, stupid, shivering rain-sodden us.

Wednesday ◆ NOVEMBER 26

There could be no better demonstration of what I wrote yesterday than the Commons debate today on the Chancellor's pre-Budget statement. It was hardly a debate, but simply political punch and Judy all over again. In other words an infinitely boring political game of Tory versus Labour. Nothing new was said, and it seemed to me to be a waste of time.

Thursday ◆ NOVEMBER 27

Alas! Disaster follows disaster. In Brazil rain and mud-slides have killed 80, with 8 cities cut off and 54,000 people rendered homeless. In Thailand ant-Government riots have closed both of Bangkok's international airports leaving tens of thousands of tourists and businessmen stranded. In India –where terrorism is not unknown – 104 visitors and local people have been killed, with thousands injured as armed terrorists bombed and shot their way into two major hotels and other installations in Mumbai. Bush, Obama and Brown have all condemned this obscenity.

OTHER NEWS: The QE 2 has berthed for the last time, and is in Dubai where it will become a luxury hotel. Of more interest to the nation at large is the story of the father who raped his two daughters over a period of years so that they gave birth to a veritable family of children. It is not just greed that stalks the asylum, it is evil. There is universal astonishment and disgust that such a thing could happen in the 21st century and in the so called civilised West.

Recession problems add to anxiety. MFI and Woolworths have both called in the Receiver, which means there will be thousands more added to the ranks of the unemployed.

In gentler waters it appears that such is the demand for tables at the Band's farewell dance that we are having to consider a second farewell. Already more than 400 people want to join us, and we have a waiting list of 140. It would seem that a swathe of mid-Scotland's chattering classes want to dance away the gloom.

Friday ◆ NOVEMBER 28

In Mumbai, India's financial capital, the terrorists attacked a café, two hotels, a railway station and a Jewish residential and business centre. Government troops continue to respond. It is a battle, with guns blazing and explosions filling the air. At least 200 are reported killed, with some 300 injured.

Today graphic accounts of the action swamp TV and Radio. There are massive explosions and fires in the enormous Taj Hotel. The terrorists were holding hostages, but by lunchtime the Jewish centre and one of the two hotels were declared cleared. The chaos continued in and around the Taj. Some commentators liken the affair to Nine/Eleven and the London bombings. There is no certainty as to who the terrorists are.

Saturday ◆ NOVEMBER 29

The mayhem in Mumbai is almost at an end. Nine of the ten terrorists are killed. Governments continue to take the view that terrorism can be defeated. Are they right? Terrorists attack wherever they choose. So we attack the terrorists wherever we can find them. But, when we kill them, others return the favour and plan more attacks. That is the actual, real world agenda. Thus, the killing never ceases and will not cease until and unless Governments don't simply talk peace but DO peace. Meantime there are daily bombings and killings in Iraq, in Afghanistan, in the Congo, indeed almost anywhere you care to look on the global map. Even Bangkok is not a happy city. Both its airports are still out of action as crowds in opposition to the Government continue the blockade. Tens of thousands of travellers sit, and wait.

Sunday ◆ NOVEMBER 30

Hope was the theme of the sermon today in Elie Parish Church, and it was also the theme, spoken and un-spoken at Quaker Meeting. It is the best four-letter word in our lexicon, but it is a useless, hollow word unless it is harnessed to a five letter word called Faith. The Meeting was utterly silent and still apart from words on hope from one Elder. Into my empty mind floated figures like ghosts who moved and knelt as if in prayer. They were distinctly seen.

Monday ◆ DECEMBER 1

FAREWELL – AND GOODBYE. AGAIN!

President-Elect Barack Obama has two children, both girls. Sasha and Malia. I was interested to note that they are to attend the Quaker school in Washington and will go to Friends Meeting every week.

This afternoon Jenny and I will drive to Edinburgh for the Monks' December Chapter. In addition to refection and verses a new Monk is to be inducted, but I don't know who he is.

NEWS: Following the battering to death of Baby P, senior officials at Harringay Council have been dismissed. The whole event has been a national scandal.

Tuesday ◆ DECEMBER 2

I do not doubt that there are heroes and heroines in the UK. Just plain, nice folk caring for their families and doing a daily honest job of work. So there are good corners in the asylum for which we should give thanks. There are also vast numbers of people who eliminate thoughts of doom and gloom, and unemployment, by playing sports, or attending sporting events. By and large as a nation we participate in sports of all kinds, and that helps to cheer us up, medals or no medals.

Overseas there is good and bad news. In Thailand 300,000 travellers who have been stranded at those airports are now starting to be able to fly home. But we should not go to Venice at present. It is knee-deep in flood water, ie: water where it should not be. And where it should be it isn't. That is in north east Brazil where there are now vast areas of arid land with no water at all because the rain forest there was destroyed.

Wednesday ◆ DECEMBER 3

It is more than difficult to find good news. In Harringay more social workers who neglected Baby P (who died from parental assault) are being dismissed. Several were earning £40,000 per annum. For inefficiency. Not only is Harringay at fault. We are being told we have a public health problem. Research reported in The Lancet reveals that one in ten children in the UK are abused in one way or another with parents much at fault, dealing out punishment to their kids which is described as being either physical, sexual or psychological abuse. And how about that monster called Peter Tobin, now imprisoned for life, after raping and killing a lovely young woman, then chopping up her body and hiding the bits. Police suspect that, over the years, he may have given the same treatment to 12 other women. Where one inhuman act is discovered there may be many more which remain uncovered. So – the merry month of December continues to develop more carbuncles to keep us aching until Christmas.

Thursday ◆ **DECEMBER 4**

Personal anxiety and, perhaps, a partial filling of my well of hope fuelled this dream. And such conceit! I found myself to be a guest at a pre-oath meeting chaired by Barack Obama who had called Republicans as well as his Democrats to sit together. Beside me was the nanny who looks after Obama's two children, and she was plying me with questions as to whether Europe would welcome Obama as the forthcoming American President. I earnestly attempted to re-assure her and said we were in fact delighted that Obama was soon to be in the Oval Office. While he would certainly have to shoulder almost impossible burdens in the USA as well as across the world we felt he was the best man for the job.

Friday ◆ **DECEMBER 5**

We await yet another Gas Board engineer to repair our central heating. It still requires attention, and today is one of the coldest this year. Meantime the media offers us extra anxieties. In Bangladesh children are being paid 7 pence an hour as they make clothes for three of our largest main street retailers. In addition high finance is brought lower by most Banks refusing to pass on the Government funding they have received to mortgage customers.

Most shocking of all is the story of Karen Matthews who kidnapped her nine-year-old daughter for money. The child was drugged and hidden but after a vast amount of time and tax-payers' money had been spent the police found her. Matthews had lived on benefit all her life (£400 a week) and had seven children fathered by five or six different men.

Saturday ◆ DECEMBER 6

Ian Haxton arranged for a dozen of his friends to join him and his wife Pat for supper in the Golf club. We obeyed the call. Good food and more than enough wine followed by coffee and brandy at £72 per couple. (I don't think I am the only club Member who is in love with ' the Stewardess' Elaine who organised the event with Ian.) She is small, and beautiful. And sexy.

Sunday ◆ DECEMBER 7

To the Parish church with Jenny, followed by coffee and a mince pie in the church hall where there was an exhibition of paintings in aid of a charity. Some good work, but a great deal of trash as well. Then it was back to the world of telegrams and anger with the media commenting on further doom and gloom.

*Unemployment (UK) has risen by 140,000 in the past three months. * Average house price drops to £31,487. * New car registrations down by nearly 40 per cent. * In Zimbabwe unemployment is at 80 per cent. The cholera epidemic is spreading. Half the population is starving and one million people have Aids. There is a renewed call for the UN to get Mugabwe removed and made to pay for his crimes against humanity – he has all but destroyed an entire nation. Meantime, in this country our economy is in free fall as we enter "a full blown global recession." What, I wonder, is all the doom and gloom doing to our hearts and minds.

Monday ◆ DECEMBER 8

Over the past few days Band member David Todd has been sending us up-dates on the numbers of people who want to come to our farewell dance at George Watsons. The latest figures show that for Friday, January 16th there will be at least 14 tables of ten, and on Saturday the 17th there will be 35 tables. So far 574 people have booked and more replies are expected. Apart from 'tickets' we have received a total of £4,650 in donations. So it seems we are up for two farewell parties. David deserves a medal for all the work he has done in mailing our lists of friends and collating results. In fact he has a medal already from the King of Norway. It means in that country he would be known as Sir David Todd! (But that's another story).

Last week the Minister (Brian) from the Parish Church called by to ask whether in his Sunday Service (January 18th) I would give a brief talk about the Quaker concept of silent worship. I replied that I would, and said I had already sent him an e-mail which, apparently, he had not received.

Tuesday ◆ DECEMBER 9

For the past three days the young people of Greece have been engaged in riot and fire fights with the nation's police, and not simply in Athens. The violence has spread throughout the land and to islands including Crete. It follows the shooting of a teenager by the police. Stansted Airport also have had problems. Some 50 'protesters' broke through security barriers and camped out on or near runways so that no aircraft could take off or land. They were objecting to the plan for the construction of an additional runway, and also sending a signal to Government about lack of action on global warming. While their action was illegal I have some sympathy with their view. There is much talk, even at this minute, between European nations concerning global warming, but where's the action? There are more aircraft flying and adding to global warming. In developing countries, as well as China and India, more factories and more cars are pouring out dangerous carbons. The madness continues. Talking is not enough. There is a widespread call for remedies now, but there are none, and it is becoming too late to save undreamed of disaster that awaits our children's children and their grandchildren.

The Monk called Father Adventus has written a brilliant verse heralding our Festival in January. It is titled 'Return to Jurassic Park' and begins as follows:

Our Era now has reached its end
The human race – without a friend –
Faces now, with no distinction,
Its quite well deserved extinction.
For the whole Earth is now used up
An orange sucked - an empty cup.

Great stuff! It continues quite splendidly…but I will not repeat someone else's lines that belong only to The Monks of St. Giles.

Wednesday ◆ DECEMBER 10

The Government declares that there are at least four and a half million people in the UK on Benefit. There are some who are either too ill, or disabled and simply cannot do a job. But there are many others who prefer the easy life, who choose not to seek work and who survive by taking Benefit and supplementing that income by doing a bit of naughty on the side. "You gotta pick a pocket or two". Shop-lifting, probably. The Government is now planning to withhold Benefit payments to those who scrounge in that way.

Tonight TV is to show a man with motor neurone disease taking his own life (in a clinic in Switzerland). I am not sure that this will cheer us up. Whenever possible I feel death should be a private family affair, but I cannot understand why suicide should be illegal here when killing someone other than yourself should be legal, ie: war, when service personnel bomb and kill people they have never seen before –- civilians, including mothers and children. That is simply senseless, random slaughter, like murder. However, in Time Past, and Present, called History, that seems to be what we in the asylum, and most other places under the sun continue to practice.

Thursday ◆ DECEMBER 11

When you see a helicopter hovering low at the edge of the sea you know it could be on an instruction course — or there might be something amiss. The other day I saw one and thought it was a practice run. But I was wrong. Gordon Izatt, who bought Chapel Green House from Jenny and her sister had, apparently, stepped out to see how renovations to the cliff along from the house were progressing. Unhappily he took one too many steps and fell over the edge on to rocks below. Fortunately someone spotted the fall and was able to summon help – hence the helicopter to the rescue. Gordon is now in hospital with cracked ribs and sundry other injuries and is in intensive care. He is at least 80 years old, but will live.

A wider view of the asylum shows that Woolworths have not found a buyer and so a great number of former employees will be out of a job, and the ranks of the unemployed will continue to grow. How can we write cards saying ' Have a happy Christmas' when so many people are without homes and/or jobs?

Friday ◆ DECEMBER 12

Cities of culture in the UK – we should feel proud of them, from London, Birmingham, Manchester, Edinburgh, Glasgow and others. Music and the Arts generally still flourish despite the credit crunch. But, unhappily, something else survives in our cities for which should feel ashamed and angry. We have a gang culture, a knife culture, a drug culture. We also have a family break-up culture which means that many kids don't get a chance to grow and to develop in a decent and responsible manner. Gang rape of young girls is not uncommon. One such incident was reported today in all its terrible detail. There have been, and will be, more that we never hear of. Are we looking the other way? My hope is that the police in our cities should be enabled to round up the gangs and not only publicly name and shame the miscreants, but also punish them. A prison sentence will not do the trick for once 'inside' they will encounter – yes, more drugs and violence. Prisons, with table tennis TV, free food and its own gang culture can do little to teach a lesson. A sound thrashing, in public, might do more to discourage rape and killing. That is a strong view for a Quaker. But at Quaker school the cane was used in extreme cases, and prefects were allowed to spank with a slipper if lads in the dormitories got out of hand. I very much fear that in our dangerous streets a prison sentence will not deter young men and women who are determined to behave in an obscene and criminal manner.

(In Zimbabwe the situation is well past danger point. It is now exporting disease in the form of cholera).

A different dismay afflicts the USA. The Senate has refused – so far – to enable the Government to fund billions of dollars to the ailing motor giants called GM, Ford and Chrysler. Bush is angry, and if these corporations are not rescued Barak Obama, once in office, will have yet another intolerable problem in his 'In-Tray.' (There is every hope that money will be found to save the motor industry).

Saturday ◆ DECEMBER 13

Cinderella. The annual Pantomime in the local Townhall after three months of rehearsals. We went along to tonight's show with the Peebles and the Glens.

Somehow it lacked the charm that we saw in last year's show, but there were some good performances, notably Dr. Gilly Thomson as Prince Charming, George Harvey known locally as Hoover 'n' Hoe, who played Buttons and sang well, and Geoff Hooper who was one of the Ugly Sisters (Francie and Josie) and was also one of the co-producers of the show. Packed houses roared out the songs and over the three nights the raffle alone raised £1,000 for the local Improvements Fund. At 10.00 p.m we adjourned to the Peebles home where Sheila and David provided six of us with a splendid meal of stovies, pies, sausages, baked beans and a four-hour flow of wines. We staggered back to our house at 2.00 a.m.

Sunday ◆ DECEMBER 14

More show biz. This evening we watched the annual BBC Sports person of the Year in which the public phones in the name of the favourite they want to win the contest. With many of the world's sports heroes and heroines on view, plus seasoned Presenters and the BBC Concert Orchestra, the show was a wonderful, heartening and moving spectacle. A feast, a congregation of superb, dedicated athletes in almost every known sport. The winner was The cyclist Chris Hoy who won three gold medals at the Olympics. I felt that the designers and producers of tonight's spectacular should have a medal all to themselves.

Prime Minister Brown was not present. He is, quite properly, in Pakistan making it clear to the Government there that he feels three-quarters of the terrorist plots that threaten the West are hatched in Pakistan. Indian leaders (en effet) say "we'll second that."

As the PM roams around, saving the world from more horrors, the double-dealing, wars, slaughter and general mayhem continue unabated. Thank goodness for the world of sport and the success of our country's stars. They give us all a breath of hope.

Earlier in the day I accompanied Jenny to her Church. A thin congregation but better than nothing. Except –alas, those hymns. So few can sing them, and although I enjoy singing, I could barely strike a note.

Monday ◆ DECEMBER 15

I caught the closing overs of the Indian Test, and witnessed a sad English eleven. They should have won this match after their brilliant second innings, but alas, the two Indian openers, plus an assured 100 from Tendulka, put the cork back in the bottle, with the loss of only four wickets. This one, they said, "is for Mumbai." Stranger things can happen. It's been snowing in Portugal.

Stranger and stranger indeed. A Wall Street banker called Bernard Madoff has literally made off with a tidy sum in a multi million Bank fraud and has just paid $10 million bail money. Several big Banks have lost out, having invested large sums with Madoff. Royal Bank of Scotland – among others – has lost £400 million. To add to the general joy world markets are reported to be falling (well, they were falling anyway, so what on earth is going on, or going off). House prices are falling still further, and the pound (£) is continuing to be worth less against the Euro.

The good news: if fewer Brits decide NOT to holiday on the Continent next year and take their holiday at home instead it could mean better business for our hotels and B&Bs. But then, even more bloody CARAVANS!

I'm a Brit – get me out of here. Anyone for the moon?

Tuesday ◈ **DECEMBER 16**

After visiting Charmian, Jenny's elderly sister yesterday it is becoming clearer by the day that very soon she will require day-long professional care. She cannot stand, or walk more than a few steps and the NHS seem to be incapable of stabilising her blood pressure or curing a cough . I think her lungs are a mess. She rang at nine this morning asking for Jenny who went to her immediately. The two part-time private carers appear to be unavailable and Peter (son) is having toe nails removed. His caring time is strictly limited anyway, as he has a business to run. One ill person can change all our lives, even in this privileged community.

Wednesday ◈ **DECEMBER 17**

This evening we were invited to have supper with David and Judy Mason in their holiday home by the sea shore. Bill and Mary Elder were also present, so the conversation flowed along fortissimo. We got into politics rather than golf and I found myself at variance with David who is very right wing and who gets a bit steamed up when talking of the present Government. Bill Elder and I take a more Liberal view. We enjoyed Judy's food and David's Port in this most hospitable home.

Thursday ◈ **DECEMBER 18**

Today we will drive to Edinburgh, find a bed with Peter and Sheila Gordon in Currie prior to tomorrow's New Club Ball where the Band will play for the last time (apart from the Farewell dances next month).

TV news reported more heartbreak for five families who have lost their sons, killed in Afghanistan. They were all super young men who believed in serving their country, and did so until they were cut down. I was terribly moved, and angry at this continuing madness and waste. Next year British troops will finally be withdrawn from Iraq. They should also be pulled out of Afghanistan in a conflict there that can never be brought to a sensible conclusion. We are crazy. We will sing Carols and say Merry Christmas. What, alas. is merry about killing and grieving. Christ – not simply at Christmastime –– offered the way of Peace, but very obviously human kind long ago decided they knew better, and have continued to make war which simply fans the flame of hatred, mistrust and grief.

Friday ◈ DECEMBER 19

We awoke in the West Wing at Currie Bank after a candle-lit supper last night with Peter and Sheila. After breakfast we drove into town to John Lewis to choose a small sofa and new bedside lamps. Lunch at La Petite Folie was disappointing, but the place was packed out and the chef was not at his best. Back at Currie a two-hour sleep, then we changed and drove down to The Freemasons Hall for the New Club Christmas Ball. We drank champagne in the lower hall with the guests who had paid £90 per head for supper and dancing. This was the Band's final fling and as we ended we were thanked by the Club chairman and the secretary. It was a bit of a noisy rabble and I was glad to get back to bed in Currie by 3.00 a.m.

Saturday ◈ DECMBER 20

Peter and Sheila were very kind and generous hosts –– but had problems boiling my breakfast egg. We had a problem with the car, rang the AA who arrived tout de suite and cured a front off-side wheel in 15 minutes enabling us to drive confidently back to Fife. Jenny hung masses of Christmas cards around the hall and on doors and lintels, and still they pour in.

In the evening we ate supper in the Golf House Club with about 50 other Members. My delightful table companion was Libby Dickson, sister- in- law to Michael Dickson who had arranged the conviviality. Libby is a schools inspector in southern England and was on her customary Christmas break with husband Niall and the family. Everyone present knew everyone else, and everyone behaved well, squeezing the most out of the familiar parish pumpery – as chattering classes do. I reminded myself how fortunate we were to have such comfort and familiar pleasures, with a roof over our heads.

Sunday ◈ DECEMBER 21

President Bush's waning Government has decided to pour thousands more troops into Afghanistan. And some 3,000 more Brits are required out there. France, Germany and Italy do not seem inclined to participate. Fifty percent of Zimbabwe's population is starving and very many are dying of disease. No festive cheer for them. The madness and disaster continues with neighbouring African countries un-caring and declining to attempt to remove Mugabe. I wonder if food and medicines from Europe are reaching those who are most in need.

Jenny wrapped presents, we decorated a small tree, wrote cards and put up a few tiny coloured lights in the bird cage.

Monday ◈ DECEMBER 22

The rush is on! The push and shove. Glad tidings of traffic jams and queues! God bless us all in this annual grab for bargains and gifts. In Heavens' name why do we do it. John Lewis in Edinburgh told me business had never been brisker, and as for other retail outlets it's a case of shoulder your way in, if you can. Where is the credit crunch now? Meantime the world's motor industry is struggling and seeking extra billions (even Toyota in Japan). So its bed socks for Auntie and a bottle of rum for Dad, and everyone wanting to walk in a winter wonderland. Except there is no snow. Just grey skies, arthritis and dyspepsia.

Tuesday ◆ DECEMBER 23

We have hung 150 Christmas cards. Fewer than last year. There must be a credit crunch after all. And not so many letters enclosed, so hurrah! We do not have to read how well teeny-weeny Wendy did in her eleven plus, and what a fab time Mary and Joe had in the Maldives as a friendly farewell before they divorce.

(I have just wished my muse a Merry Christmas, and the above is the response I received). I just wish I could say Happy Christmas to my neck and right shoulder, but unhappily they are severely distressed. The pain and lack of mobility is such that I have had to ask Suzie for some help later today.

Wednesday ◆ DECEMBER 24

It appears that I have injured my right shoulder (and upper back) and have quite a lot of pain. Jenny went to a children's Christmas service at St. Michaels, but I decided to lie low.

Thursday ◆ DECEMBER 25

A very social day. After Church Peter and Sue provided the annual post–breakfast taster of champagne, scrambled egg and smoked salmon. We then went up to Cadgers Way with our presents for lunch with the Dicksons. More champagne, then a splendid lunch with the family – Libby, Niall, Bobby, Clare, Carolyn, Ralph, Colin, Andrew, Jenny and Jools, and little Isla who is a beautiful child. After coffee presents were exchanged. Among other items I was given the Reuters book 'The State of the World.' It is a magnificent illustrated tribute to the work of those intrepid journalists. We gave a variety of presents to all there assembled, including the silver bracelets for Caroline and Clare. We returned to Cadgers Way in the evening and met a roomful of relations including The Cashmere Queen. On learning that I was unable to move my right arm she attempted massage, mainly to my head and neck. When, tired but well refreshed I climbed into bed there was an aura of sweet per-fume that she must have transferred to me during that massage. I had Heaven scent dreams. Before slipping into the land of the unconscious I reflected on that large family and their kindness. They are so much more than good neighbours, always treating us as part of their family. That was the way, even in their early Glasgow days.

Friday ◆ **DECEMBER 26**

A different kind of Christmas in – was it –- LA? Father Christ-mas called by the home of his former wife, shot nine people, set fire to the house and then shot himself.

We asked neighbour Peebles and family to look in for drinks before lunch. Then Sheila and David asked us back for supper which included a remarkable red cabbage dish. It was so deli-cious we decided to buy red cabbage and try the recipe tomorrow. And again, we were knocked sideways by the kindness and warmth (and love) of our neighbours. If such open generos-ity and plain decency could be repeated throughout the land Britain would be the kind of paradise Old Testament prophets longed for.

Saturday ◆ **DECEMBER 27**

Bought a melon, more cheese and some Parma Ham for the sup-per we are giving on Monday for the Dicksons, Rosses and Euan H-W. We plan a pheasant casserole –- and noisy conversation. These are strange, dog days as we flop around waiting for 2009 which wise men say will be worse than this year. They are warm-ing up for it in the Middle East where Israel forces have attacked Gaza, killing 270. There will be no peace in the Holy Land until Israel withdraws its settlements in Arab country. Maybe in 2009 Barack Obama may help to make a peaceful change there. It is diplomacy not guns and bombs that is required, as people of goodwill pray for a change of heart that will not savage the hearts and minds of innocent families who simply wish to tend their vines and olive groves.

Sunday ◆ DECEMBER 28

To Church with Jenny who was on the door and also reading a Lesson from Luke Chapter one. Minister Brian was on duty somewhere else, so we had a stand-in who built his sermon, and the service, around angels whom he called VIPs. It rang bells with me because of course I am keen on angels.

And now, this year of grace 2008 is drawing to a disastrous conclusion. Four senior C of E Bishops are attacking Gordon Brown for his fiscal policies. Things have reached rock bottom when they play the political blame and shame game. What on earth are these alleged spiritual leaders doing? Their attention, their words and their actions would be better turned to the deplorable slaughter in the Middle East. Why are they not on their feet calling for peace, instead of playing Party politics. I am disgusted. I suspect the Bishops, like communities here at home, have had to hear so much of war and suffering that they are becoming numb and deaf to tide after tide of violence. This is not a good omen for the year 2009. Will Hope be the next fatality?

Monday ◆ DECEMBER 29

The sun is blinding today. It is 80 F in the Bird Cage. It cheers us up, and we need cheering. Israel has spent a third day literally destroying Gaza. More than 450 killed and 1,400 injured. This is a war crime, a sickening and terrible disaster. The hospitals cannot cope. There are problems in the Middle East that may never be solved. The whole area urgently needs a make-over. Otherwise we may as well all die, for humankind seems now to be hell–bent on self destruction. Let the ice age come again. And the hot and burning age also, so that planet Earth can be wiped clean of humans. Then new life, trillions of years ahead, can start again from the minute worm in its salty tomb. If it does not, then human life will end up as a joke and the laughter of the spheres will echo endlessly among the empty, starry wastes.

Until then, we will have supper with our friends. Champagne and canape. Melon and paper-thin Parma Ham from Mellis. A main course of pheasant casserole with seasonable vegetables, including the famous red cabbage. Before this I will serve a small broth of sweet potato and coconut. Jenny will provide oranges in cointreau and a lemon souffle and we shall have Stilton and other cheeses on offer. The Margaux I had so carefully nurtured is lousy, so I will pour a decent country red from the south of France and a steely Cab. Sauv. Dare we think of Gaza?

Tuesday ◈ DFCEMBER 30

Last night, I am relieved to say, was a great success. Michael and Dorothy, Colin and Elaine and H-W were in sparkling form. They loved the food, drank the wine and left at 11.00 p.m. As Jenny and I cleared up we decided to do the same again tonight for Alan and Jean Glen and David and Sheila Peebles. They are all such faithful neighbours.

Today the sun blazes as Jenny takes Libby Dickson to Pilates and I make more sweet potato and coconut broth, and re-set the table.

Only one more day to record in this Journal. As I set down the last words I badly need to be hopeful for 2009 and know it will be difficult. My suggested answer to the many dire problems that anger and dismay us are not the solutions that most denizens of the asylum would want to hear. If we wish to save others as well as ourselves in the so called civilised West we require nothing less than a moral and spiritual renaissance. This means the practice of Christian values not simply by the committed few, but by all sorts and conditions, rich and poor, the fortunate ones well as those downtrodden or sorely under privileged. To walk cheerfully over the earth, as George Fox said, answering that which is of God in everyone, is a sensible way to proceed. It challenges us to keep a balance, and attempt again and again to walk that high wire of Faith.

Wednesday ◈ DECEMBER 31

Last night with our friends and neighbours we ate and enjoyed the repeat supper. Conversation flowed as freely as the wine. Jean informed me yet again that I was "spoiled" by my wife, and

Sheila cross-questioned me on what my family did during the Second World War (Owen worked with an electronics company devising blind landings for aircraft, while Alan served with The Friends' Ambulance Unit in Southern Italy).

This evening Jenny and I will join a table of eight which Carolyn McDonald has organised in the Golf House Club, so it is there that we will bid 2008 goodbye. Later we will call in for "a swally" with Harry and Kay Murray. No doubt, after our feasting, we will sleep soundly, not forgetting our prayers for all those in the asylum less fortunate than ourselves. I could well do without the guilt and the goodbyes, but it is time now for Auld Lang Syne, and time to make ready for The Auld Reekie Band's two farewell dances in January when we hope to add to the £20,000 we have raised. So the message must be, after 2008 is done and dusted, hang in there, and hang on to the big word 'Hope.' A man called Barack Obama is at hand.

Stop Press

Clearly it was written in the stars. It had to happen at the tail end of the year. After playing for dancing in the Club for some twenty minutes, Band leader Ray Elrick left his post to visit the Locker Room. There he fell and damaged his head. Peter Gordon (Dr) was summoned to assist. An ambulance arrived to take Elrick to hospital. The dancing ceased until Peter joined the remaining two musicians and took his place at the keyboard. It was debated whether I should go and fetch my drums to help out, but two ambulances had blocked my exit. Thus it was that I had no choice but to re-join the party and, finding a big tray, was given several glasses, a water jug and two desert spoons with which to tap out a rhythm. I am pleased to record that there was general cheering, and everyone started kissing and dancing again until the bells rang in the New Year.

Printed in the United Kingdom by
Lightning Source UK Ltd., Milton Keynes
138130UK00001B/111/P